IRISH PRIDE
AMERICAN COURAGE

IRISH PRIDE
AMERICAN COURAGE

WILLIAM M. O'HARA

Published by
BUSCA, Inc.
Ithaca, NY 14851
Michael D. Cooper, President
Copyright © 2000 by William M. O'Hara

Library of Congress Cataloging-in-Publication Data
O'Hara, William M.,
IRISH PRIDE – AMERICAN COURAGE /by William M. O'Hara

Integrated Book Technology Co., Troy, NY

Printed in the United States of America

ACKNOWLEDGMENTS

This book could not have been accomplished without the untiring and devoted assistance of my daughter, Shannon O'Hara, and the unending support of my wife, Ceil.

The book is dedicated to Catherine Neary O'Hara whose life provided the inspiration for us all.

IRISH PRIDE
AMERICAN COURAGE

Book 1

ONE

THE IRISH COUNTRYSIDE resembled a scene from heaven in the morning with a light mist giving way to bright sunshine, leaving a sparkle from the dew on the grass. The land abounded with ancient castles, gravesites and stone markers from earlier times. Cows, sheep, donkeys and chickens shared the fields. Brown trout were plentiful in the rivers.

The cottage of Martin and Mary McGuire Neary was one of many farm homes at CastleBar, County Mayo. Located on the Atlantic Ocean side of the Island, the area was very severe on farmers trying to make a bare living from the poor soil. The area had great stretches of moorlands. Farming was the main occupation. They worked hard just to stay alive.

It became apparent to the Neary girls, Mariah, Catherine (Kate), Margaret (Maggie), Ellen and Rose that they would have to move. The choices were England (heaven forbid) or America. The first to sail to America was Mariah who found employment and sent for her sisters.

Kate, Maggie, Ellen and Rose traveled to New York by way of Queenstown. They were processed through Ellis Island. All were nervous and apprehensive going to a new land and a different way of life but they were leaving poverty and hunger with no opportunity for betterment.

The year was 1898. Kate Neary was a stunning young lady of 17 years with light red hair, a beautiful complexion and a sparkling smile. On board ship, she acted somewhat reserved and was on her best behavior. Kate was known to have a devilish side to her, which surfaced a number of times.

Aboard the steamer were several tall, blond, handsome Swedes. One of these young men was attracted to the Irish colleen. One morning he got his nerve up and approached her at the ship railing. Unable to speak English, he did try to say "Good morning". Kate felt she would help. Making use of the Gaelic language, she taught him how to say "Pogamahone", implying that this word stood for "Good morning". They practiced for a little while and he was very pleased.

The young Swede tipped his hat and walked down the deck lined with several huge Irishmen. To these fellow passengers, he tipped his hat, smiled, and said "Pogamahone". He was nearly assaulted. One threatened to toss him overboard. Later he learned the Gaelic word provided by the attractive colleen meant "Kiss my A-" (lower extremity).

The passage was reasonably smooth. The Neary sisters traveled to Utica, New York and Mariah had living quarters for them. The sisters were employed in a large knitting mill on Broad Street. Each worked six days a week from 6 AM to 6 PM. Wages were $3.00 per week. They took room and board at a residence on Milgate Street. For all of them, this was a radical change to the Ireland they

2

left with its open fields, the sea, and many friends. Many were the times they would bring food including bread, cheese and dry oatmeal to their rooms to satisfy hunger.

Gradually they got over being homesick and became used to the new foods, styles and different ways of living. They attended St. Agnes Church. Soon, they joined friends at dances and gatherings. There was a large Irish population on the East side. Those who emigrated earlier were always trying to assist the new arrivals.

The work routine inside the mill was severe for young people who recently came from a land where out-of-doors was so natural. One of the mill supervisors was most overbearing. In fact, he was downright nasty. He took delight in berating employees for the slightest infraction and he never let up. However, it was common knowledge that each workday, right after his noon lunch break, he would sit on his high stool overlooking the factory floor and take a nap. He held his pen in hand as if to post the production ledger but, in fact, he would be asleep.

One of the employees he picked on was Kate, partly because she was so well liked by everyone and also because she made no mistakes.

The supervisor's pride and joy was his large, waxed handlebar mustache. One day, while all the workers on the production floor looked on, Kate carefully and slowly reached up from behind and, with her scissors, snipped off one side of his prized mustache. She quickly returned to her machine and carried on her duties as usual.

Word of her action spread through the workers in the entire mill. A short time later, the supervisor stirred, looked around the production area briefly and then took out his can of wax. He applied the wax to one side of his mustache and with some degree of panic, tried to locate the other side. He reached for his mirror and let out a yell. He immediately strode to Kate's machine. You could cut the air with a knife. Kate appeared to be engrossed in her duties and ignored the supervisor, a look of complete innocence about her.

"I know it was you that did it and you'll be fired!" he told her.

Further, he threatened to get her when she left the plant at the end of the shift. That night, about a dozen workers walked out and surrounded Kate insuring her safety as she left for home. They continued to do so for the following weeks. Kate was both the talk of and the hero of the plant. The only question was, "What's next?"

During this period, many events took place in the outside world that would affect the country. Newspaper headlines of February 16, 1898 announced the explosion and sinking of the battleship Maine in Havana Harbor. It was war with Spain as of April 21, 1898. The ending of the war was announced in newspapers of August 13, 1898. In Utica, the Saturday Globe, February 28, 1898 carried the headline: "WILL AMERICA'S GUNS BE TURNED ON SPAIN?" One article in this issue carried bold type: **"Not In Thirty Years Have We Been So Close To War"**. (Reference here is to the Civil War.)

About this time, Kate met James B. O'Hara who had come to America around 1897 from Ennis, County Clare, Ireland near the River Shannon. They met in the usual, formal manner at a house gathering. It was weeks before Jim ventured to ask Kate for a date. Finally he did, and they went for a boat ride on the Erie Canal. Those simply were the good old days.

Kate had a great desire to see her parents, family and home one more time. She made a return trip to Ireland and was the center of attention. Kate traveled the countryside to visit her relatives and friends. Finally, she bid farewell to all at home for the last time and sailed once again to America.

One by one, the Neary sisters married. On June 1, 1904, in a ceremony at St. Agnes Church, Kate married Jim O'Hara. They moved into a small house on the very edge of the city's East side.

Mariah married Michael Malone and they set up residence on Hammond Avenue. Maggie married Joseph Morrissette. Rose married Daniel Cronin and they moved to Kirkville, near Syracuse where he was a foreman for the New York Central Railroad (NYCRR). Ellen married Daniel Goggin and they moved to Holland Patent to operate a farm.

For the first time since living at home in Ireland, Kate had an opportunity to bake and cook. She was determined to be a success. In order to be proficient, one had to work at it, and she did. One day, Kate started out with a bushel of apples, flour, lard, sugar and rolling pin and, working with a wood fire in the kitchen stove, began to make apple pies. It took her all day until she was satisfied with the results. She produced the absolute best apple pie that was possible. Immediately and in later years, her delicious apple pies became well known and were always in demand.

Kate and Jim's marriage was blessed with children and the first-born was Helen. The second born, James, became very ill with pneumonia and died as an infant.

Jim traveled to St. Paul's Church, Whitesboro, where

he spoke to the pastor about buying a cemetery lot in Mount Olivet. In so doing, he selected a twelve grave lot. The pastor remarked, "Why so large a lot?" Jim is said to have replied, "Because I have a young wife."

Children did begin to fill the house. John was the next arrival. He was followed by Catherine (Kate), Martin, Mary, and James. During these early years, Jim worked as a crane operator in a nearby foundry. This was a 6 AM to 6 PM out-of doors job in all seasons and in all kinds of weather. Later on, he became employed at the Forest Park streetcar garages.

TWO

LIVING ON THE East side of the city was ideal. There was a mixture of Irish, Italian, Polish and other nationalities, all very friendly. They got on very well together. Nearby were two large public parks known as the Proctor Parks. At the end of Bleecker Street was that magical place known as Forest Park, a well developed amusement area.

Forest Park was a well-kept, colorful operation. It featured entertainment attractions on stage, a roller skating rink, dancehall with live music, roller coaster, train rides, merry-go-round and a ride known as "The Whip", along with games of chance. Admission was $ .10, as were the rides.

When they became of age, John, Catherine and Mary worked at the Park as cashiers after school and during summers. Also at the park was a great baseball field. This attracted many teams. Babe Ruth is reported to have appeared at one of the games.

On Sunday afternoons, a large group of Irishmen would gather in the nearby park to talk, play horse shoes, compare notes on jobs, perhaps take a refreshment or two (or three) from the ever-present beer wagon. There were usually upwards of 200 in attendance and each wore a suit, shirt, tie and sported a straw hat or derby. They were workers, tradesmen, some merchants and a number of professionals, 95% Irish. This was their day off from work. For a group photo, the front rows would recline on the grass while the taller men stood in the back. Many had become US citizens while others were awaiting citizenship.

One of these was Jim O'Hara. It is duly noted on his certificate of citizenship, written out in fine penmanship:

"James O'Hara, under date of 31st Day of July, 1903, formerly a subject of the King of Great Britain, was admitted by the County Clerk, County of Oneida, State of New York to be a citizen of the United States of America."

A great attraction for all were the fireworks, held around Memorial Day (then known as Decoration Day), the 4th of July and Labor Day. Hundreds of people gathered along Bleecker Street at Culver Avenue to watch the display, set up in the vacant area across the street. Visitors would sit on the front lawn and mill about at this social event. Later, they walked home in the dark, perfectly safe, with no fear of muggings or robberies.

Father Glenn, pastor of St. Agnes Church, would take a stroll with his dog, Prince. He always stopped at the O'Hara's to speak with Jim and partake in a cup of tea and a slice of pie.

Early summer mornings were always a great time. Walking through the streets of the East side, pushing a large two-wheeled cart was a robust woman who called out in a loud voice, "Escarole, escarole!" From her garden she had vegetables and fruit. She could be heard a city block away. Kate would look over the offerings and buy some items for the table.

On Friday mornings early, the fish truck drove slowly along the streets loaded with fresh fish packed on ice. It was a common practice for the driver to blow a bugle to announce his presence. One day, on Oscar Street, he let out a blast on his bugle. A man who was sleeping on the second story porch had just returned from the Army. Hearing the bugle, he startled and jumped over the railing to the street below. He landed on the lawn, apparently unhurt.

Kate seldom purchased fish from this truck, but would send someone on the streetcar to the Jones Fish Market on Pearl Street for her Friday meal requirements. Friday was a strict fast from meat and Kate was so strict on this rule that she would not even give the cat a bit of meat!

A few blocks distance was the Black Bridge. This was located at Tilden Avenue and Lansing Street and crossed over the West Shore tracks of the NYCRR.

A group of young teenage boys hung out at the bridge and were known in the neighborhood as the "Black Bridge Gang" under the leadership of one Ernie McGuire. Though for the most part quite harmless, this devilish group was full of pranks and could become most brazen. They were suspect of having stolen tomatoes from neighborhood gardens and around Halloween, they were at a peak of activity.

The Black Bridge was located close to the Blandina Street streetcar loop, which was the end of the line. The trolley would go around the loop. If the light at the top of the signal pole was on, the motorman waited several minutes before leaving. In this manner, he would meet the next streetcar at a place where two short tracks allowed them to pass each other. Otherwise, it was a one way track.

On more than one occasion, someone climbed the pole and turned the bulb off. The streetcar would take the loop and immediately speed down the street toward the city. Approximately ten minutes later, the streetcar that just sped away would appear, backing up slowly, bell clanging with the second streetcar following it to the loop. This would disrupt the travel of many people trying to get to work or home. It is alleged that members of the Black Bridge Gang took turns climbing the pole. The city police would show up and ask questions of the neighbors but no one was ever arrested.

The regular patrolman for this neighborhood was Pete Malone, Mariah's son. His regular beat included the Black Bridge. More than once, Officer Malone was intimidated, if not challenged by Ernie and his gang numbering seven or eight. They called the Black Bridge their very own.

Pete Malone was short in stature but solidly built and very quick on his feet. As he approached the bridge, he would call out to the gang to disperse. One time, after they refused to move along, Malone waded into the group, nightstick coming down and around. It was short and furious. Skulls and shins could be heard to crack. Four lay on the bridge deck, stunned. Malone held one against a bridge support with his nightstick. The others ran away. Neighbors telephoned for help which quickly arrived.

Although shaken up with some facial cuts, a black eye and a torn uniform, Malone insisted on completing the rest of his beat. He was heard to say, "I'll keep a lookout for the two that ran off." Pete never backed away from a challenge to his authority as a policeman. He had his club and a whistle, which he rarely used. Police did not carry a gun at that time.

Pete was a regular visitor to Kate's kitchen where he was served hot tea and apple pie. If he was not on duty, he might have something a bit stronger. Everyone liked hearing of his latest adventures. They would pass along the news of the day sitting around the dinner table.

Kate always had a bountiful meal on the table for both family and several boarders taken in to make ends meet. Over the years, it was not unusual on a spring day to see a dozen apple pies cooling on the open windowsills before they could be cut. In fact, the first pie theft probably took place around this time.

Zito's gasoline station was located on the corner of Culver and Bleecker Streets. Frankie Zito had a weakness for apple pie. It is alleged that he removed one hot pie. Looking out her kitchen window, Kate saw him juggling something hot and eating away in an attempt to devour the evidence. Having a big heart, Kate always baked an extra pie, just in case.

Over the years, Kate's apple pies continued to be sought by friends, neighbors and of course, relatives. One evening at dinner, a boarder did not have room for pie after two servings of the main course. He asked if it would be permissible to take a piece out with him (an early carryout). Kate told him, "You can eat what you want at the table but cannot carry any food away." He was last seen forcing down the pie.

One day, Kate was very busy getting food ready when she slipped on some flour in the kitchen and had a hard fall. Dr. Fred Douglas determined that she had a broken leg. He applied splints and ordered her to three weeks of rest. Rose traveled from Kirkville to help her sister. Kate gave the instructions and directions to keep traffic moving in the house.

Kate told Dr. Douglas, "Tell me what I owe you, and payment will be made soon." Dr. Douglas noted that Jim was laid up ill in another room. He looked around and said, "For my fee, I'd settle for one of those apple pies cooling on the window sill." And so it was that the cost of Kate's medical treatment was resolved with a pie. For many years, Dr. Douglas remained a good friend of the family. He served as Mayor and then in the US Congress. Later, his son, Dr. James Douglas, stayed in close touch with the O'Hara's and proved to be a real friend like his father had.

The boarders living at the house were variously employed. The East side of the city was home to many industrial activities including machine shops, a foundry and several small manufacturing firms. Savage Arms Corporation was located on Turner Street and employed hundreds in the production of sporting arms. During war years, many additional workers were hired.

Yet another two-wheeled wagon was pushed along the East side streets. A friendly little man sold lemon ice on a stick for only $ .01 each. He also sold popcorn and candy. He was probably the very first "Good Humor" ice cream man. Where in the world could one purchase a cooling refreshment on a hot day for a penny?

IRISH PRIDE
AMERICAN COURAGE

———————————

Book 2

THREE

A GREAT BLIZZARD spread over upstate and covered the city with a blinding mantle of white. Snowdrifts were even with porch railings. The only traffic movement consisted of streetcars that appeared out of the blowing snow with headlight and cow-catcher probing through the night. They looked warm and cozy, all lit up. Passengers kept warm from the heat of two potbelly stoves in each car.

It was February 1925; the days before snow plows or sanders. One trolley called "The Sweeper" would push a rotary broom wheel to sweep the car tracks. Another streetcar had a small plow out front. Together, they worked hard to keep the tracks open for traffic. This was actually the only cleared path for traffic and was used by autos and pedestrians.

Down the street behind The Sweeper drove Dr. Quinn. He had to park his car in the streetcar track and then dash into the O'Hara residence at the corner of Culver and Bleecker. Here, he delivered a baby boy. This took some time and, meanwhile, several streetcars full of people were backed up waiting. The passengers were warm but impatient and kept looking out the windows. Finally, Dr. Quinn

15

came out, waved to the cars, and drove off into the storm, allowing traffic to move again.

The great snowstorm and below zero temperatures could not diminish Kate and Jim's happiness. They named the new family member William, who became known as "young Bill" or just plain "Billy".

The family occupied the first floor of this large residence. The second floor rooms were rented out to boarders whose income helped since Jim's health did not allow him to work steadily.

The new arrival was cause for celebration and, appearing like magic, were several bottles of Irish whiskey for a toast or two. It also fortified those heading outside to clear away snow that blocked doors and drifts that piled part-way up the windows.

One of the boarders, a night watchman at the Winship Trunk factory next door, dressed for the cold with scarf, boots, heavy jacket and a lunch bucket slung over his shoulder. It had always been his practice to dash out the front door, rain, shine or snow, and leap-frog over the porch railing. He then would run across the lot to the factory rear gate.

Out he dashed on this blustery night, over the railing, immediately disappearing in the snow bank. It took six or eight husky men to dig him out, retrieve him with a heavy-duty rope, and get him back inside. This rescue effort was followed by lots of hot tea and more of the Irish (for medicinal purposes only). There was no watchman on duty that night.

Things finally settled down for the night while the temperature was severely cold. Smoke from the chimney was blown away by the wind but everyone in the house

was reasonably warm with the coal-burning furnace going full blast. The old house had no storm windows. Drafts
were steady and strong. By morning, the insides of the
windows were covered with a thick frost. It was not uncommon to awaken and find a thin line of snow inside the
windowsill.

Sunday afternoon was the gathering time at Kate and
Jim's. Friends and relatives stopped in for card games
and "Forty Five", a popular game at the time. Sunday was
the day off from the drudgery of the job. The men all
worked in factories or foundries or on the railroad or streetcar line. The dedicated card players were devoted to win-
ning each and every game. No money was exchanged
since no one had any. They played for points. Kate would
make tea, serve pie, or, if desired, one might have something stronger.

Two card groups of four players each were in constant motion. At one table were Kate's brother, Tom Neary,
Patty McMyler, Tommy Cunningham, and Jim O'Hara.
While Jim had been ill off and on, no one could keep him
from these games. At the second table were Timothy
Smiddy, Tom Horgan, Bill Hogel and James Cobb. A spir-
ited group they were.

Tom Neary came from CastleBar, County Mayo. He
was about five foot, ten inches, and built as solid as a rock.
He had dancing eyes and a bushy mustache. He smoked
a pipe that was so strong it could bring tears to your eyes
even when unlit. Tom's workday began at 5:30 AM as a
fireman at the Clark Knitting Mill. He walked to work
and spent his full shift shoveling coal by the ton into the
boilers that fed the plant. Tom was a very convincing individual. After telling a story about Ireland, he would

look you straight in the eye and say, "That's the way it was, by God."

Few, if any, ever questioned him on proof or details. More of Tom later.

Patty McMyler, another native Irishman, was also built solidly. He was known as a hard worker. When Neary and McMyler traveled together, no one in his right mind would challenge them.

Tommy Cunningham came to the US to earn enough money so he could return to Ireland and buy the farm of his dreams. Eventually he did. He worked at the Skenandoa Rayon Mill. The working conditions were very poor, and more than once he would need to take a day off for his eyes to recover from the chemicals. Tommy was a most friendly, outgoing type with a very heavy brogue. He got along with everyone except with his Chinese laundry man.

Jim O'Hara was about 6 feet, 4 inches, slim and showed signs of hard work and endured periods of illness. His crane operator job out in the cold had deteriorated his health. He was quiet and easy going.

This first card table would get hot and heavy about mid-afternoon, when a glass of straight whiskey (no chaser) was served. It was noted that soon thereafter, cards would be misread, the noise level increased and challenges of "renege" (cheat) could be heard.

Not to be outclassed by Table One, the second table of players was most colorful to say the least. Bill Hogel, who worked at the NYCRR roundhouse, was a bit on the robust side. Bill could eat the food of two or more men, day in and day out. In fact, he had been admonished by Kate at the dining room table for taking all the food. At dinner one evening, Hogel devoured what he thought was his bowl of soup, placed in front of him. Actually, it was gravy for the dinner table, but no one had told him.

Suddenly, one day he got into real trouble with Kate because he left his job. Asked why, he stated, "I'd just as soon stay at home where it's warm, and play cards with the other boarders." The others were out of work. Kate demanded he go and beg for his job, which he did, and went back to work.

Tom Horgan, a retired farmer from near Sangerfield, was boarding for the winter. A distinguished man in his late 70's, he dressed sharp, had a beautiful, full mustache and was always a gentleman. One morning just before Christmas, he came down for breakfast of oatmeal, eggs, toast and coffee. He was in a hurry. Tom planned to ride the trolley downtown and take the train home for the holiday. Kate wished him a pleasant Christmas and offered him a glass of spirits (homemade). He accepted.

From under the kitchen sink, Kate poured from a gallon bottle. As was the custom, no chaser was offered. Tom turned this full water glass on end and drank it all. Suddenly, he clutched his throat and gasped loudly, "My God, Kate, what was that stuff?"

Quickly looking under the sink, Kate immediately realized what had happened. The whiskey was located next to a gallon of bleach for the washer. Tom got the bleach instead of the good stuff.

He dashed from the kitchen to his room and brought out his insurance policies. In a rasping voice, he said, "I want the farm to go to my daughter, and tell them I went to communion last Sunday." He then began praying at the kitchen table.

Kate was laughing so hard that she was unable to offer any help but finally gave him a mixture to help him bring it all back up. Shortly thereafter, having recovered, he bid farewell. This time, he accepted a glass of the real stuff, but only after personally checking the bottle twice. Down it went, then out to the streetcar and he was off for the visit. Tom lived to about 98 years.

Another player at this table was Timothy Smiddy, a very serious, quiet fellow (when sober) who came from County Cork. He landed first in Boston where he and his brother worked taking care of the carriages of businessmen visiting the stock exchange. Tim left Boston for Utica while his brother remained in Boston and became friendly with several stockbrokers. He built up a sizable fortune from his stock tips. Tim became employed by the city working in the Parks Department.

An early riser, Tim reported to work at 5 AM to freeze the ice skating rinks. Since the temperature might run from 5 degrees to 5 below zero, his breakfast consisted of hot coffee and a pint of whiskey to fortify himself. For lunch, his bucket held him over. Dinner included meat, potatoes, vegetables, bread, tea and, of course, apple pie. Then he was off to bed at 7 PM to get ready for another day.

Tim was to be watched at the card table since he was a sharp player. When he was not sober, he would demonstrate a 180-degree change in character, acting in a forward mode, extraverted and one to be reconciled with. His birthday was March 17, St. Patrick's Day, and he lived to be 87.

James Cobb was the fourth player. He was a neighbor, retired, a stately gentleman, a sharp card player and aged about 78. Cobb was totally deaf and it was necessary to shout to him whenever he would forget what was trump card.

He attended 7 AM Mass at St. Anthony's every day, except on Sunday when he attended the 9 AM at St. Agnes Church. During winter months, his walking up the streetcar tracks through the snow caused problems. Being deaf, he claimed he could not hear the trolley, bell clanging, right behind him. More than once, the motorman, Cornelias Goggin, would poke him very gently in the shins with the cowcatcher and this took considerable skill by Goggin. Mr. Cobb would react by shaking his cane at the streetcar.

One morning, he actually gave the trolley a couple of raps with the cane but then stepped out of the way. For this, Con Goggin would give him a wave and a smile. A devout man, Cobb then got back into the streetcar lane and continued on his way to church.

The card players would discuss some of the main issues of the day, problems at work, and any news about Ireland. All of their information came from letters and the newspapers. Their questions concerned the English and what they were doing now to cause problems in the old country. Most belonged to a local organization called the Ancient Order of Hibernians (AOH). Dues were $2.00 per year. It was suspected that dues monies and other funds were sent in support of Irish Republican Army activities and put to use by the IRA. For some years, young Bill would look upon all English with reserve because of so many stories of hardship told during the Sunday card games. But not all conversation involved the English.

Tom Neary usually had a story or two. He would recall an incident that took place near his home at

21

CastleBar. The room would become very quiet as Tom described one spring day that brought a great amount of rainfall. His father had taken his donkey, loaded with bags of grain, to a mill for grinding. The rain increased to a downpour. The journey took most of the day.

As his father was returning, the river had spilled over the banks and was flowing over the small bridge. It began to get dark and the path was slippery. It was a hard task for man and beast to approach the crossing.

The poor man was ready to give up. He offered a prayer for help. Suddenly, lighted candles appeared on the donkey's ears, lighting the way over the bridge and offering safe travel through the storm to his cottage.

In telling this and other stories, Tom would do so with great conviction and sincerity finishing with, "And that's the way it was, by God." He would look you straight in the eye as he concluded. Nobody would question him after such an effective presentation. However, young Bill wondered how the candles could have remained lit in the rainstorm.

Early on Sunday, Kate would take young Bill on the trolley to the 7 AM Mass at St. John's Church. They sat at center aisle, five or six rows up. The carfare was $.10 each way and Bill rode for free. For each Sunday he attended Mass, young Bill would get an ice cream cone from his father. Also on a given Sunday, the McTigue family would travel from Troy, NY to visit the O'Hara household. Sometimes, Aunt Maggie and her family would also visit and this would be an all-day event with the Kodak kept busy. Aunt Maggie lived in Albany.

The card games were in full swing one wintry Sunday afternoon. At about 2 o'clock, there was a pounding on the front door. It was a wild day from the start with blowing snow and very cold temperatures. Kate opened the door and there stood a young girl, a neighbor, crying, with no boots and no coat.

Her friends Mary and Catherine quickly took her to the kitchen. She told of running from her house, a full block away, after her father had harmed her. Worse, he would follow her with his big German shepherd dog. Young Bill was rushed out the door with his sled to go over her tracks in the snow. He did his best to block out the tracks as the blowing snow helped him.

Suddenly, out of the snowstorm, the angry father appeared with an enormous dog. He demanded of young Bill, "Have you seen my daughter?" Bill just went on playing in the snow. The man went up on the porch and pounded on the front door. This time, Jim opened it.

The man demanded, "I want my daughter. Bring her out!" The dog was straining on his leash.

When the man became insistent, Tom Neary, Patty McMyler and Bill Hogel stood next to Jim and persuaded the man to leave and told him not to return. He later was seen near the street, watching the front of the house. Finally, he left.

Later that evening, after dinner, the young girl was taken across town to safety at the home of her relatives. In the months following, the German shepherd became a real threat to everyone. He was allowed to run loose and was considered dangerous.

On his day off, Tim Smiddy liked to take a stroll up the path and through the fields near the house. His mind would be far away on County Cork and his home. Tim was by far the slowest moving person in the boarding house. Suddenly, about 100 yards in the distance, the German shepherd appeared. With a snarl, he took off after Tim, ready to bite. Several witnesses reported that Tim exceeded the track record for the quarter-mile in his dash to the back door, making it by inches.

Late in the evening, when most everyone had retired and young Bill was supposed to be sleeping, he could see the light on in the kitchen where Kate was making up lunch pails for the next day. Finally, one could hear a clicking noise throughout the quiet house. This was Kate winding up the kitchen clock, the last job of the day. The next day started at 5 AM.

The house was always neat and clean, thanks to Catherine and Mary. They would do most of their work on the weekend. Since there was no vacuum cleaner, they would sprinkle snow on the rug and sweep it into the rug to pick up the dust. Cleaning day might be the same day that the Coakley Coal Company truck would back up to a cellar window and deliver about 10 ton of coal. The coal would go down a chute into the coal bin while everything upstairs got a fresh coating of fine coal dust. The furnace used 20 ton per year. This was the famous "Blue Coal" as advertised. It became "blue" as the driver sprayed a blue liquid over the coal bags at the time of delivery. Kate would always invite the driver into the kitchen for something to warm him up on a cold day.

In those days before television, computers and the Internet, radio and the movies were key sources of entertainment. The Irish always liked to gather for an evening of dancing. Many a Saturday night, this took place in the O'Hara home. A fiddler was hired for the evening at the prevailing wage of $2.00. He was allowed all he wished to eat and drink, though this was not always the best arrangement. He was expected to play from 7 PM to midnight.

To prepare for the dance, all furniture was removed from the living room, except for straight chairs along the walls. With about ten couples dancing an Irish reel or a square dance, the dining room floor would begin to sag. That's why, early Saturday morning, four stalwart young men would go up to the nearby West Shore Line NYCRR tracks and tap out a few railroad ties from underneath. These would be placed vertically under the dance floor for support. The day following the dance, the ties would be slid back under the track but the spikes would not be driven back in, since this would make too much noise. The old railroad track inspector could never figure out how the ties had become loose.

The dancers comprised about fifteen couples. The music was lively. Beer, homemade whiskey, sandwiches, tea, coffee and all types of pies were served. Almost everyone was on best behavior. There was no reserve in the dancing. The couples would go all-out. The fiddler was given a short break at 9 o'clock. Sometimes he would disappear. Someone would go and fetch him from the saloon two blocks away. The floor always held up, thanks to the NYCRR. At midnight, the dance ended since the last streetcar came by at 12:20 AM. The dining room was then put back together for breakfast.

At another social event, again on a Saturday night at the O'Hara house, the same group would gather to play cards for prizes. The game was "Forty Five". Preparations would begin about a week ahead of time. The prizes consisted of ducks, chickens, a gander, a small pig and sometimes a turkey. These were all under the care of young Bill and were kept in the yard where he fed and watered them. Of course, all this took place prior to the invention of food freezers.

Kate had everything ready the night of the card games. Everyone was in a festive and competitive mood. The ladies wore their finest frocks. The men all wore suit coats and neckties. Men played as partners and individually against each other.

Near the end of one such evening, Tom Neary and Patty McMyler were tied for the most points. It was the last hand of the last game and the winner could name his prize.

They were playing on a fragile card table of the type that folded up. McMyler pounded his last card on the table and shouted, "I've got you now!"

Not to be outdone, Neary shouted, "The hell you have!" and with great force, brought his trump card down with a fist going right through the table up to his wrist.

No one moved. McMyler shouted, "You reneged!"

Neary replied, "To hell I did, I've got the trump card!" Everyone bent over and looked under the table and, sure enough, Neary still held onto the ace of hearts, the key card!

Kate lost the table. Everyone had a great laugh. Neary selected a plump hen as his prize. His sister, Mariah, won a duck. She chided him on his selection. Neary answered, "My chicken is twice as smart as your duck."

The group all went out to ride the last trolley home. Was all the excitement over? Not quite. When the streetcar stopped, the pig got away and everyone scrambled after it, including the motorman. Once the pig was caught, they boarded the streetcar with their live prizes. The 12:20 ran slightly behind schedule that night.

Young Bill was glad the stock had departed. He had watched the events of the evening while sitting on the staircase, looking through the spindles. No one noticed he was up so late. Those adults sure carried on.

That Thanksgiving, a big turkey was bought and turned over to young Bill for care. It was placed in the basement since it was too cold to leave out-of-doors. One evening about 7 PM, young Bill went to feed the turkey but it was no where to be found. He called for help and everyone in the house, family and boarders, searched the surrounding field and neighborhood. After all, this was Thanksgiving dinner. After a thorough search, no turkey could be found.

Returning to the house where the lights were still on in the cellar, the silhouette of a turkey could be seen in the window casement. He had been up there all the time! Thanksgiving dinner was assured.

On summer evenings after dinner, Jim often took young Bill to Proctor Park and sat under his favorite elm tree. Surrounding them were acres and acres of lawn with the beautiful smell of fresh-cut grass. The parks crew cut the lawns with horse-drawn cutters. Jim and young Bill would walk to the horse barns with a few wild apples and visit with the horses. On occasion, they strolled over to the Masonic Home grounds and chatted with some of the residents who were also enjoying the evening. There was no automobile in the family at this point so it was either walk or take the streetcar.

Each evening at about 6 PM, young Bill would deliver a carry-out dinner to the night watchman at the Winship Trunk factory. The watchman stated he was soon to be married and would be away for a few days and to cancel his dinners. Later, he returned his dishes to the boarding house kitchen. Some of the boarders began to heckle him about marrying a much younger girl.

Mr. Sheehan, the watchman, spoke up. "Actually, that really is not a problem, you see. I'm going to marry her mother." This terminated all conversation on the subject.

With the great amount of food that was consumed, groceries and meats were required on a daily basis. One icebox was available to store only milk, meat and leftovers. Milk use was limited to tea or coffee or on cereal. One could have a little butter or jam/jelly, but not both. It was discovered that one person had buttered a slice of bread, turned it upside down and added jam to the top. He received a rap with the broom handle as a reminder of the rule.

Kate designated young Bill as grocery deliveryman. With his wagon, he would cover the five blocks to the LoGalbo grocery store at the corner of Bleecker and St. Anthony Streets. This was known as the second LoGalbo. There were three LoGalbo stores. The first was operated by Russo and the second by Severio. Carlo LoGalbo operated the third. Kate did all of her business with Severio. However, on occasion, Bill would visit the third LoGalbo and he was delighted to do so. Here they sold steamship tickets and had color posters of huge sailing ships. Most tickets were sold for travel to Italy. They did a brisk business.

Bill dreamed that some day he would travel the oceans of the world on a large ship. Little did he know that he would someday set sail, but it would be on a troop ship rather than on a passenger liner.

Mr. LoGalbo and Kate had a credit arrangement. Each visit resulted in an entry in a little "trust" book. At times, the balance in this trust book would become the subject of considerable discussion over the telephone. The problems were usually resolved. This was during The Depression and money was extremely scarce. Prices were much lower then. Sugar sold for $.02 a pound. The sign outside Zito's gasoline station read, "7 Gals. for $1.00". Hot dogs were $ .10, served on a bun with mustard or ketchup free.

With Kate, the preparation of food came naturally. She would start very early in the day baking pies, biscuits and rolls. To get ready for Sunday dinner at 12:30, she might place two pork loin roasts side by side in the oven. The fire was fed by hard wood and the stove lids would at times become cherry red. Vegetables on top of the stove might include beets, cabbage, corn or peas. Potatoes were served at every dinner. That was it for Sunday. At 5 PM anyone interested might have tea, a sandwich and pie. Interestingly enough, there were no tossed salads, wine, beer or whiskey served with meals, but whiskey was known to have been served between meals.

Some very amusing people came to the door making deliveries. These included the breadman, iceman, milkman, mailman, eggman and others. The breadman from Wind's Bakery in Whitesboro would park his truck at the curb and come in and help himself to coffee. On a day when it was below zero, Kate furnished him with a water glass of whiskey (homemade). She would do the same for the mailman whose nose could match that of Rudolph the Reindeer. More than once, the breadman could be seen sitting in his truck, window down, getting his bearings before the next delivery…if he could only remember his route. Likewise, the mailman would step out into the cold morning and then lean against the porch, re-sorting his mail deliveries and re-checking the next stop. The milkman escaped these problems. He delivered at 5:30 AM and was always on the go. His name was Bill Zeiter, a most friendly person.

About this time, Tommy Cunningham announced that he had saved enough to return to Ireland and purchase the farm he'd always wanted. There was a fine gathering of all his Irish friends, fellow card players and people from his work. In their own way, they had a great celebration and Cunningham was a little overwhelmed. He probably never thought he had such a wide association of friends. Finally, one morning, he took his old battered travel case and after a going-away drink, boarded the streetcar for the railroad station. He sailed from New York City.

It was about a week later that a man wearing a pigtail and round hat knocked at the door. Kate answered the door and greeted him as if he were a next-door neighbor. It was at this point that the caller identified himself in broken English as Mr. Cunningham's laundryman. He only knew Cunningham as "Mr. Tom".

He next picked up a large basket of clothing, showing Kate. When told that "Mr. Tom" had sailed for Ireland, the man exploded. No one could understand Chinese. That was a good thing, since he was very angry. Cunningham never did get along with his laundryman so before leaving, he went around and picked up all sorts of old torn clothing including cast-offs from the other boarders. He ordered these all to be repaired, cleaned and starched and he would stand the expense, whatever it might total. The laundryman could be heard making derogatory remarks about "Mr. Tom" as he went up the street.

FOUR

JIM WAS CONFINED to bed for many weeks, losing ground each day. He had actually been ill over a long period of 18 years. Young Bill stood by his bed and tried to talk to his father when he was awake. Then, on October 19, 1930 at 4 AM, Jim passed away with his family at his side. That morning, when he awoke, young Bill was told that his father had gone to heaven.

Early that morning, a black crepe was hung on the front door, as was the custom. Young Bill went outside to play and saw Mr. Winship, owner of the factory next door, coming to work. Mr. Winship always stopped to talk with the boy. He asked about the crepe.

"My father died," young Bill answered. Mr. Winship expressed his sorrow and said he would stop later in the day, which he did, offering his help. Mr. Winship was a true friend to the family.

Starting that day, and for the next two days, the family was visited by friends, neighbors and dozens of relatives from far and wide. They brought great amounts of food for the family and boarders. The men stayed in the kitchen while all of the women kept to the dining room.

Some remained awake all night, which truly made it an old fashioned wake. In addition to all the food, there was an abundant quantity of refreshments.

The morning of the funeral was bitter cold. Aunt Mariah stayed at the boarding house to care for young Bill. She prepared food and coffee for those who would return from the cemetery. The house was stone quiet except for the high wind. Aunt Mariah, young Bill and two cats, Whitey and Tom, were the only occupants. Mariah was very kind and explained the day's events, answering questions to the best of her ability. She was very much like Kate.

FIVE

FOLLOWING THE FUNERAL, Kate let it be known that she planned to remain at that location and continue her work. This was a brave move. The year was 1930, one year following the great stock market collapse. The Depression was being felt at all levels. Unemployment was very high and money scarce.

At this time, Helen was married and living with her family. At home were John, Catherine, Martin, Mary, James and Bill. Catherine was employed as a secretary at Savage Arms. John worked in the Stores Department at the NYCRR in Malone and later in Utica. Martin, Mary and James were in school and young Bill was getting ready to attend St. Agnes.

Just a few days after the funeral, a Welfare Department woman called at the house. Neighbors had reported a widow with children and hard times. Kate had never asked for assistance. The representative said that the icebox, telephone, newspaper and other items, including the radio, would have to go.

Kate explained that she did not request welfare. The woman became quite antagonistic. Kate took the woman by the coat collar and out the front door she went, notebook and all. No welfare requested, none desired.

It was tough going. The boarders took any work available, from shoveling switches at the NYCRR yards to picking apples. They searched for work daily. Some worked in the worst of conditions. It was most difficult to stay ahead of the "trust" book at the store. Board and room were $6.00 per week. Everyone in the house pulled together and they made it, telephone, icebox and radio notwithstanding.

Kate tried selling sandwiches and pie to the factory workers at Winship and to those working on WPA projects nearby. Although few workers had any money, enough bought so that it made a financial difference in the house. Young Bill pulled his wagon loaded with food, arriving just before lunchtime. He couldn't make change, but no one took advantage. The weeks flew.

About this time, John married Esther Marriott and they settled into an apartment over in the city.

The close proximity to Proctor Park allowed for recreational activities in all seasons. In the summer, cool walks through the woods, lawns and along the creek. This brought relief on hot days. In the winter, there were hills for sledding and skis for excitement. At that time, skis had only toe straps, no harnesses or ski poles. This made for some interesting, quick downhill decisions.

The "Starch Factory" creek flowed through the park. At an isolated spot, some young lads made a dam for swimming. This became a great spot, available free to all. Norman Rockwell would have enjoyed painting this group.

Saturday morning might find young Bill and a few of

his friends on a hike beyond Proctor Park, across Welshbush Road and up into the hills. They would make a small fire and fix lunch of Kate's stew beef and coffee. Food prepared over an open fire always tasted great. This took place near Perry's Cave, a rock out-crop in the side of a hill. The alleged train robber, Perry, was thought to have buried his treasure nearby. The boys never found anything of value but did carefully search on each hike.

Wild apples and berries made a great snack after lunch. Although the lunch was always filling, they were as hungry as tigers by the time they arrived back home. Each would have a sunburned nose and a face full of freckles.

Catherine and Mary shared a room on the first floor, front, just off the porch. They could be heard laughing over incidents from the workday.

One evening they were looking out the bedroom window with the light off. A large lilac tree stood in front of the window. There was a car parked out front. The horn would blow softly every so often. The occupant, a man, kept looking at the house. Earlier that day at work, a supervisor had been bothering Mary for a date. After ignoring him as long as possible, she finally said, "OK," just to get rid of him. The supervisor was in the parked car. Finally, he drove off.

The next day at work left much to be desired but the girls had a good laugh and the supervisor never bothered Mary again.

As young Bill moved along in years (6, 7, 8), both Catherine and Mary were very attentive to him. They took him downtown and to magical places like F.W. Woolworth's toy department or the Robert Fraser department store, both located on Genesee Street. They went to

35

Forest Park and Proctor Park for summer walks or to ski in January and February. Maybe he would take up music. Mary was quite accomplished at the piano and let him sit on the bench while she played her favorites including "Deep Purple" and "Stardust". Another popular song was "The Sweetheart of Sigma Chi". In years later, Bill recalled sitting at the keyboard with Mary, especially when this music would come over the radio.

On the first Friday of each month, Catherine, Mary and young Bill walked to the 7 AM Communion service at nearby St. Anthony's Church. They usually greeted old Mr. Cobb there. Some mornings they would meet Bill Zeiter, still delivering to his milk customers. It was necessary to bring the milk bottles inside from the cold since the cream at the top would freeze and push the round cardboard covers off the bottles. These were the days prior to homogenized milk.

Mary graduated from St. Agnes School as both class president and valedictorian. That summer, she worked as a cashier at Forest Park. In September, she became a freshman at Utica Free Academy and took the Commercial course. She joined the Psi Rho Signa Sorority and attended her first formal dinner at the former Hotel Martin.

Mary began receiving invitations to many activities and met a lot of new people. This had all come to a halt during the third week of October when Jim passed away. She was close to her father who spent a lot of time with her on writing and reading. He always took great interest in her school activities.

In the school year that followed, Mary spent much more time on her studies and less on social activities. During the following summers, she continued working at Forest Park. In addition, she was a great help to Kate.

But Mary did find time to attend football and basketball games. She dated several young gentlemen at school. One of these was Jack Ward, who was a star on the UFA basketball team. In her senior year, she devoted almost all of her energy to her studies.

It was a very long walk to and from UFA and Mary would become very hungry enroute home. She said that everything reminded her of food. Even the blowing leaves reminded her of cornflakes.

In a prepared paper dated 1934, Mary elaborated on family history, her life up to that time and her goals and ambitions for the future. She hoped to gain employment as a stenographer and progress to secretary. This was at a time when openings were very scarce. Her avocation was to be an author, writing fiction. From her income, Mary planned to take her mother to Ireland for a visit and then tour Europe. She was dreaming and planning.

It was apparent that, for her age, Mary was considerably ahead of her time in her thinking, both career-wise and in her general outlook. She thought nothing of challenging a statement or known fact. However, she had the unique ability to do so without being antagonistic. Sometimes she was not satisfied with a standard answer that would satisfy most others.

A few blocks away on Tilden Avenue lived some O'Hara cousins. Mary and Michael O'Hara had five children: Anne, Lillian, Mary, James and Michael, whom everyone called "Joe". In the dead of winter, it was a great relief to stop at their home for a few minutes to get warm on the way home from school. It was about twelve blocks each way.

The name "O'Hara" was well known and well re-garded on the East side. However, the actual family name was O'Hare. In processing through Ellis Island, the busy officials read and recorded the name as "O'Hara" and no one was going to challenge immigration. One might end up on a return ship to Ireland. Therefore, James and his brother Michael began to put an "A" on the end of their name while their cousins processed through, still known as "O'Hare". But then, what's in a name?

At Memorial Day, then known as "Decoration Day", Kate and young Bill would ride the streetcar to Whitesboro. They walked from Main Street up the hill to Mount Olivet Cemetery with a few geraniums to plant at Jim's grave. On their return down the hill, there was a spring that pro-vided a cool drink. Near the trolley stop was a Mom and Pop store where one could purchase an ice cream or Es-kimo Pie for $ .05. Either was worth a million on a hot night. This trip was made a few times during the sum-mer. Sometimes, a ride would be offered and they were never too proud to accept.

About this time, a new face appeared on the scene. Catherine had met Bill O'Connor at Savage Arms. He was outgoing and friendly. Bill was a recognized area speed ice skater who trained year-round and entered in a number of meets. His other interests included skeet shooting and bird hunting. He dressed to the fashion of the day and drove a Dodge. Catherine and Bill began to date on a regular basis. Incidentally, O'Connor was hooked on apple pie.

Young Bill started work at an early age. The Winship general foreman would walk up in the field where Billy was playing and take him for a visit to Mr. Winship's of-fice. The factory was building some new strollers and, although overweight and oversize, Billy would sit in them to test for durability. If the stroller made it with him in it, it passed inspection for production. Sometimes the strollers simply fell apart. In any event, he would receive $ .25 for his services plus any treats available in the office. This income was a good start at savings since admission to the Rialto Theater was only $ .10.

The Sunday afternoon card games continued, but less frequently since Jim had passed away. A new Philco tabletop radio brought in entertainment such as the championship boxing matches, Jack Benny and others. "The Shadow" was very popular on late Sunday afternoons.

One interesting radio program was the Father Coughlin Show, a broadcast originating from Cincinnati. Somewhat controversial, Father Coughlin would take a strong stand for or against some issue of the day. His choice would automatically become the position of the house members for the week. His position had to be the right one. After all, who would question or argue with a priest?

The heavyweight boxing matches were the greatest attraction. Some dozen people would be gathered in the dining room to listen to the fight. All faced and stared at the radio as many would later with television.

Another radio announcer, Walter Winchell, held everyone's interest with his opening remark, "Good evening, Mr. and Mrs. America at home and all the ships at sea." Winchell was very caustic and hard-hitting. He poured it on for the full fifteen-minute program from 9:00 to 9:15 PM and covered people and events of the time. Portions of his communications were no doubt factual, some questionable. But few listeners doubted him since he sounded very convincing. And besides, he talked so fast.

The radio brought the "Lone Ranger" program week-days from 5:00 to 5:15 PM, a critical point in the day. No sooner would the heroes begin chasing the outlaws than a request would come from Kate to "Run to the store and back". Or, worse yet, be ordered to turn the radio off and get to the dinner table. There was no justice. The Lone Ranger took second place.

The dinner table was an education in itself. Family and boarders would recall the day at the railroad, mill, shop or office. One of these was Mr. Clark, a NYCRR engineer who worked in and around the Utica "Round-house". He drove a huge steam locomotive and moved disabled units around this repair facility. It was located at the foot of Culver Avenue and Broad Street. There was a long wooden bridge going over the main line tracks to the repair yard. Mr. Clark casually said that he would try someday to have young Bill pay him a visit at work. Perhaps he would like a ride in the locomotive.

The next afternoon young Bill proceeded down Culver Avenue, over the footbridge and on with the search for Mr. Clark at the train yard. Walking on a busy path alongside the locomotive tracks, he spotted Mr. Clark going by in the cab of his locomotive. Clark leaned out the cab window, took one look and came to a quick stop. He jumped down the steps and hauled young Bill up into the cab to safety. After admonishing him, Clark told Billy to stand back and hold onto one of the cab fixtures, and then went about his work. It was a completely terrifying experience to say the least. The steam locomotive made sudden starts and stops, was very loud, hissed, rattled, snorted, was very hot and practically scared a young person to death. A fireman in the cab was busy shoveling coal into the fire. With the fire door open, it could have been over 95 degrees. Finally, after about two hours, Mr. Clark finished work and escorted Bill safely home. He promised not to tell, provided Bill never again visited the rail yards.

Arriving home late, Kate was waiting impatiently with a long store list and a short time schedule. She took one look at the railroad soot and grime. In no time, she extracted a confession on the events of the day. Out came the yardstick with several well-placed whacks followed by hot water, soap and clean clothes.

What followed was one of the fastest shopping trips on record. While the grocer was cutting the meats, Bill loaded groceries into his wagon. In the days that followed, he erased one career path from his planning - that of a railroad engineer. Incidentally, Mr. Clark never did tell.

One weeknight, more than a dozen musicians arrived at the house. Martin played saxophone in a band, and the boarding house was selected for practice. It was fun. Everyone enjoyed the free entertainment except when the band kept repeating the same music for the refinement of mistakes. At 10:30 Kate had enough and told them to go home, but gave them something to eat first. The band held together for some time and played at dances, weddings and parties. For playing 7:30 PM to midnight, each musician received $2.00 payment.

Bill had many friends including Jack Dwyer and Walter Glozak. Jack lived on Ontario Street. His grandmother, Mrs. Walsh, had a fine little apple orchard. The apples were always fresh and sweet. Walter and Bill had old bicycles. They began to live with adventure by exploring new, distant streets, too far away to travel on foot.

In the mid 1930's, the period of Lent was a busy time at St. Agnes Church. The Stations of The Cross would be held on Friday evenings starting promptly at 7 o'clock. The church was full. Bill served on the altar along with his many friends, one of whom was Ambrose Byrne. The altar boys had two leaders, Art Holdridge and a fellow named Flagler. Both made sure everyone could recite the prayers and hymns in Latin one hundred percent without exception. A full choir and an organist presented music for The Stations.

The altar boys included some of the pranksters from the Black Bridge Gang. These angels wore high white starched collars, white surplus with black trim. Each carried a lighted candle in procession with the pastor and his assistants. One could be easily overcome by the aroma of burning wax and incense. It felt like being in heaven for a short time. The ceremony was meaningful to all. The Stations of The Cross was simply the place to be Friday evenings during Lent.

The altar boys who resembled angels during the ceremony slowly walked off the altar and out of sight. The instant they exited the doors heading downstairs, they did a 180-degree turn-around in character. Friendly shoving, punching, a trip here and there and just all-out hell-to-pay until the sisters came downstairs. Then immediately, there was peace and tranquility. The sisters usually had access to a pointer. This round, wooden, two-foot long, rubber tipped item was used in classrooms (1) to point out objects on the blackboard and (2) for discipline. The latter was accomplished when the sisters determined that a violation had taken place. Only the sisters seemed to know all the rules and regulations. They were quick to apply the penalty. This usually consisted of several sharp whacks to the palm of the hand with the pointer. To this day, anyone who ever attended a Catholic grade school can easily be identified from the pointer marks still on the palm of his hand.

During this time, the boarding house rooms were full and this was quite a cosmopolitan group.

One of the boarders, Max Strogel, had come from Germany. He was a machine operator at Savage Arms. Max, who spoke broken English, said that he came to the US from Germany only long enough to earn money, then planned to return and open his own business.

Max kept to himself, was known as a loner and one day quit his job. He rented a farm at nearby rural Frankfort Center. His quick departure was the talk of the house. A week later, a letter arrived for him from Germany. Kate was planning to return it to the mailman. But young Bill and Walter volunteered to deliver it on Sunday by riding their bicycles up to Max's new place. Actually, they wanted to see where he had gone and find out what he was doing. There had been some talk about the boarding house regarding Max and Germans in general. At that time, Adolf Hitler was pressing German neighbors and flexing some muscle in Europe.

The boys rode several miles into the country and located the farm being operated by Max. When they arrived, Max was out in the fields. The temptation was just too great. They peeked in the windows expecting to find a short-wave radio or some type of spy equipment. There was nothing.

Soon, Max returned and offered them food but they had brought lunches with them. Max opened the letter and became very excited. It was an offer of employment and an invitation to return to Germany. He was immediately interested.

Max traveled to Germany that fall. Some time later, through his former associates, it was believed that Max was lost during the German invasion of Norway.

SIX

In July 1938, Kate moved the family to 1005 Steuben Street. This was a lovely neighborhood at the time. Elm shade trees, quiet neighbors and big homes surrounded her rented three story brick home. All the boarders made the move with Kate and, with more rooms, she took in some additional boarders. City buses traveled this street, having just replaced the streetcars.

In this new residence, Bill had a room on the third floor in the back. He instantly missed his friends, the fields, the park and even the chickens and ducks. However, he retained his East side newspaper route, both daily and Sunday deliveries.

One of his immediate decisions concerned a school for the fall. Bill had completed 6th grade at St. Agnes. It was a tug of war between St. Francis de Sales and Utica Free Academy. He picked UFA junior grades and entered the 7th grade in September. This school offered music and Bill had started taking trumpet lessons.

Kate's new boarders made up an entertaining bunch including Joe Roddy, a solid and most sincere Irishman. He worked nights at the NYCRR preparing freight cars for shipments. Sam Hutchinson and Eddie Lannon worked in the NYCRR Stores Department. Fred Freeman, a former lumberjack, worked at Savage Arms. Tim Cahill was employed at the Skenandoa Mill.

One very unusual character was Luke Easton who worked at the Kennedy Sports Company. He was built like an ox. Luke was always late for dinner but could eat enough for three people. He had been asked to slow down on the food intake. Board and room were still only $8.00 per week.

One evening, Luke arrived to find his dinner plate already fixed. He immediately began to devour his food. Inside a huge stack of mashed potatoes was a very liberal helping of red-hot homemade horseradish, freshly ground. Luke had been seated behind the table. All water glasses had been removed from the table.

Starting with the potatoes, he began to wolf down his food. Suddenly, he jumped up, his face red and eyes ready to pop out. He nearly overturned the dinner table trying to get to the kitchen for water.

Absolute bedlam followed. No one finished the meal. No one could stop laughing. Tears flowed with laughter. Luke finally recovered and returned to finish his dinner, making sure first that no one had fixed his plate in advance. Joe Roddy claimed credit for this caper. This was entertainment that could never be bought on the outside.

Catherine and Mary continued to help Kate around the house while working at Savage Arms. Martin and Jim also worked at Savage. Helen, her husband Joe Roth and children Jean, Beverly, Ronnie, Brian and Anne resided at Dearborn Place.

During the summer of 1938, tragedy struck the family. Jean Roth and her neighbor, Mary Murphy, ages 12 and 14, drowned while on vacation at Oneida Lake. They had fallen into a channel in the lake. The girls had just graduated from Our Lady of Lourdes School.

At this time, news from the outside world began to darken with war fever. In Europe, talks started between Neville Chamberlain and Adolf Hitler over the Czech crisis. On the other side of the world, Japan continued to invade China.

All of these developments seemed a million miles away from the lives of the O'Hara family. The world was quickly shrinking and soon these events would affect everyone.

The social event of that summer was the marriage of Catherine to Bill O'Connor. They moved into an apartment on upper Elm Street.

Mary continued with quite a bit of social activity with many friends from work, attending dances, parties and visiting. She traveled to Orchard Beach, Maine or to Troy on summer weekends and would take the Old Forge ski train in the winter. She dated but did not seem to have a "steady". Telephone messages for her covered the wall.

Kate loved to go to the Knights of Columbus and play bingo on Friday evenings. It was the event of her week. On occasion, she might win $50.00. One night, she won a Toastmaster toaster. She was so angry over not winning cash that she tossed the Toastmaster into a trashcan near home. Upon hearing this, Mary dashed out and retrieved the toaster. It lasted in the household for years.

With her baking and cooking, Kate always had a full boarding house. The apple pies helped. In the early summer, her dessert menu included homemade sliced biscuits covered with big red strawberries along with a heavy layer of homemade whipped cream. This always brought requests for seconds.

With the responsibility of raising a family and concentrating on simply getting by, Kate always rented. However, she now began to look for a suitable property to own. How this was to be financed had not been ironed out, but one had to start somewhere. Planning ahead, Kate began her search.

In the summer of 1939, Catherine and Bill O'Connor drove Kate to the New York World's Fair for a few days. It was her first overnight trip in many years except for a trip to a shrine in Quebec. She enjoyed her short vacation.

Bill was now a student in the UFA Grades. Much to the consternation of the neighbors, he continued his trumpet lessons. He was admitted to the UFA Junior Band.

He began work as a part timer at George Reichardt's Drug Store. Bill took the job left vacant when Bob Sweeney joined the Navy. He made deliveries, served up ice cream on the soda fountain and, under the direction of an older employee, Jim Amrhein, learned how to make chocolate syrup. The drug store was a busy place and time went by quickly. The pharmacist would spend a great amount of time making up prescriptions by mixing chemical ingredients. Large, impressive bottles of different colors sat on the shelves. Some were rarely used.

One winter morning, boarder Stanley Dobler returned home from his second shift job and discovered the house almost full of smoke. He woke everyone up and the fire department was called. The fire had started on the second floor in old Mr. Cronk's room. He had apparently gone to bed with a lit cigar. Mr. Cronk suffered complications and passed away. The Utica firemen were great in every detail. Everyone pitched in to clean up from the smoke and water damage and in no time things returned to normal.

A new boarder, George Gregory from Monticello, New York, arrived on the scene. Employed at Savage Arms, George was a sharp looking man with blond hair and deep blue eyes. After high school, he completed a machine training course and was a natural born mechanic. He was very good at set-up and operation of machinery. He read diagrams and prints and explained complex mechanical matters in simple terms. He could look over a mechanical problem and recommend a solution. George took flying lessons after high school.

George worked long hours and his favorite entertainment on a Friday or Saturday night was seeing a movie with Bill. Later, hamburgers and coffee along with discussions on flying and the war took up their time.

One evening at the dinner table, George explained his ideas on how to improve the synchronization of an airplane machine gun firing through the aircraft propeller rotation. Some at the table scoffed at his ideas, however the arguments died down as George carefully addressed each question. It was clear that he had given much thought to this subject and he planned to forward his ideas to proper levels for consideration.

One Saturday morning at about 7:30, George drove Bill up to the old Utica Airport where he was in the final stages for his pilot's license. It was about ten degrees below zero on a February day but with brilliant sun shining. Visibility must have been twenty miles.

George introduced Bill to several people, one of whom

said, "Over this way." Later, he learned that George had identified him as a prospective student. Bill was totally unprepared for the next event.

Before he knew it, Bill was seated in the back of a two passenger Piper Cub and was barreling through blowing snow in the bright sunshine heading toward the far end of the runway, frozen solid with snow and ice. The small yellow plane lined up for take-off and it was then that Bill realized they were taking off on skis!

Before long, they leveled out at two thousand feet. It was incredible, beyond words. The sight of the frozen canal, the city and what looked like dollhouses. The NYCRR tracks and road network leading to the city were clearly identified. The sensation of his first flight had a profound affect on Bill. He simply could not believe his good fortune of flying, no less on skis! The ride was over in fifteen minutes and was not without a few bumps and air pockets, reminding Bill of the eggs, toast and coffee at the diner earlier that morning.

The plane circled back and approached for landing. The glare was so great one could not tell if the ground was one thousand feet or ten feet down. The pilot brought the little plane down right on target with no bumps. They taxied up to the open hangar door.

Bill expressed his appreciation for the ride but had to ask one question: how did the pilot know the height coming down for a landing? The pilot said he watched his altimeter and added that he would consider the shadow near the hangar to double-check his height. Bill watched George fly solo and complete his qualifications for his license that day.

It was very soon after this that George went into the

Army Air Force and lost contact with Bill. All hoped his ideas worked out and that he would move safely through the critical times ahead.

In English class the following Monday, Bill's assignment was to write a short composition of an interesting happening over the weekend. Bill wrote of his first flight and received an "A" grade. However, the teacher, Miss Mary A. Micucci, called Bill up to her desk and quietly asked if this had been made up or if it really took place. Bill told her all about the morning, the weather, George and his first solo flight. She was convinced. Later, she taught Bill second year English.

Although the United States was not at war, European news was followed daily through the newspapers and on the radio. War news was the topic of conversation everywhere. While there was no fear, there was apprehension about the road ahead for many young people.

In the meantime, life went on. Bill joined the West Utica Boys Club Band and attended practice every Monday evening with his friend, Bob Miller, who also played trumpet. The band marched in city parades and performed at special events.

The Boys Club Band was selected to lead the parade for Opening Day at Doubleday Field, Cooperstown on June 10, 1939. The band lacked a piccolo player. Band director Jack Galloway "borrowed" one from another band just for one day. The piccolo player was older, short in stature and could pass for one of the Boys Club members. This caused some resentment among the regular members. All the trumpet players vowed to drown out the piccolo.

Down the main street of Cooperstown marched the band in bright blue uniforms, capes and hats with ten trom-

51

bones up front. Typical class "A" level march music including "The Stars and Stripes", "Washington Post March", and "King Cotton" were presented. The spectators were wall-to-wall. The band never sounded better after a full winter of indoor practice and parade ground practice marching. The band was given a great reception. However, try as they might, the trumpets could not drown out the piccolo which had a very high range.

Following the parade and ceremonies, the band members had a picnic lunch, a swim, attended a major league baseball game, their first in Cooperstown, and had a great day overall. It was a memorable event, well remembered in later years by all who participated.

It now became time for Bill to graduate from paper routes and the drug store position and move up in the world. He was accepted as an usher at the Stanley Theater which had some 2,300 seats. He worked weekends and one school night. His salary was $6.00 per week ($5.94 after Social Security) and proved to be both entertaining and educational.

Name bands including Artie Shaw and Cab Calloway appeared. Broadway plays and productions were on the schedule in addition to the latest movies. One of the major productions was the Ballet Russe de Monte Carlo, a professional touring company with a Russian ballerina performing Swan Lake. Bill was impressed with the variety of talent. The theater would usually be filled to capacity. People traveled far and wide to attend.

One Friday evening, theater manager Andrew Roy and his assistant George Laurey asked Bill if he would travel to Rome the next day to distribute posters for the Stanley. The Cab Calloway Orchestra was due the next week. This would be Bill's first expense account trip.

The next day was a cold, windy March day with rain and sleet. Bill boarded the Rome bus with fifty to sixty posters and free passes. In downtown Rome, he called on small shops, stores, restaurants, barbershops and filling stations requesting shop owners to display a poster in their front windows. The rain soaked his raincoat as colors from the posters ran unnoticed. One merchant offered to dry Bill's coat with heat from his stove. Bill took lunch in a sandwich shop. At 4:00, he boarded a bus back to Utica.

His expense account, as submitted:

Transportation	$ .70
Hamburger	.15
Coffee	.05
Apple Pie	.15
Total	$1.05

Kate was not impressed with Bill's business activities. She pointed out that, in addition to getting drenched, the raincoat needed cleaning and this cost would be deducted from the expense allowance. However, Bill had found the day to be one of great interest. In later years, he recalled the simplicity of that trip to Rome compared to his business trips for General Electric visiting major cities while balancing airline schedules, meetings and long hours.

Bill moved up to Senior Band. Not bad, since he was only a freshman. Social activities came to life with summer band concerts and movies and, in the winter, toboggan outings on the Parkway slopes. Saturday football games with the UFA band playing at half time and the Friday night dances at St. Francis de Sales School were highlights of the week.

On September 1, 1939 the nation's newspapers reported the German invasion of Poland. The September 17, 1939 headlines described a fierce battle had begun as Poland was invaded by Soviet Forces.

At Thanksgiving time 1939, Martin married Evelyn Fischer at Our Lady of Lourdes Church. They took residence in an apartment on Faxton Street. In the years to come, their family would consist of Michael, Martin (Marty), and Mary Ann. Martin continued in his employment with Savage Arms.

Kate was kept very busy baking and cooking with all of her rooms rented. Across the street, a house had just been renovated under an FHA Program. Although it was being rented, the home was put up for sale. The house had a new furnace and offered more room than Kate's boarding house. Kate discussed her intentions to buy with attorney Michael Malone and Addison White from the Utica Savings Bank. She scraped up the down payment and the transaction details were completed. After all those years, finally a homeowner.

In July 1940, Kate's family moved into their new home. What made this relocation interesting was the fact that all the boarders moved their own possessions and bedroom furniture - all three floors of it. However, some complication arose involving the fact that the family from Kate's newly purchased residence was moving into her old residence and they also had three floors of furniture. Fortunately, it was a perfect summer day and the move progressed quite well. Joe Roddy, who worked nights, actually caught a few hours sleep in the middle of all the action.

The move completed, Kate had supper prepared in her new home at 5:00 PM. Everyone was dog-tired but happy to be in the new house. Meat, potatoes, vegetables, apple pie and coffee helped restore them to life.

In the fall of 1940, James left home when the National Guard was activated. He and many others marched down the street to the NYCRR station and shipped off to Fort McClellan, Alabama. Later, James married Mary Schrader and in the years to come, their family included James, Ellen, Dianne and Ann.

Mary frequently invited her friends to the house. These were young people from the Savage Arms office. Weekend dances, picnics and gatherings brought everyone together. Mary began dating Al Radley who later became a New York State trooper. Although Mary's social activities seemed to increase by the week, she always managed to have time to help Kate.

Bill and Mary became highly efficient in the matter of after-dinner clean up, including the dishes for some 24 people. Speed resulted in some broken dishes and Kate had to put her foot down. These were the good old days before the dishwasher machine. After the evening dishes, Mary would settle things by having Bill dash to the nearby drug store for an ice cream sundae carry-out. For only $.15, one got a large scoop of ice cream covered with strawberry, pineapple or chocolate and topped off with real whipped cream. One never heard of calorie count. At least, no one worried about calories.

Now 16, Bill obtained a permit for a junior operator's license. Mary was very patient in teaching him how to drive. Kate just threw her hands up. Off they would go in Al Radley's 1939 red Ford convertible. It was usually Proctor Park or a quiet neighborhood for practice.

The NYS "Brownie" giving the driving test was

Charlie Judge from Clinton. He asked Bill why he drove with his right shoe off and he answered, "I can get a better feel for the gas pedal which only requires very little pressure for the car to accelerate." Bill passed his driving test.

Mary and Bill got along fine. She was not domineering. She was a good listener and would make suggestions, be it a course at school or some other matter. Bill, on the other hand, took great pleasure in provoking Mary, as a brother should. This ranged from practical jokes to spraying her with the garden hose while she sat in the backyard sun chair. She took it all in stride and, in fact, handed it back in kind.

SEVEN

MARY WAS A very independent thinker who might be regarded as somewhat of a renegade for that time period. Once her mind was set, she simply did not take "No" for an answer. She would strongly reason with people to sell her point of view, always short of being argumentative. Part of this attitude may have developed from Catherine's constant advice, which was very conservative. Her mother was also inclined to be reserved, and after considering these points of view, Mary would speak her piece or do her thing, sometimes leaving both Catherine and Kate astonished.

It was about this time that Mary left Savage Arms, accepting a position as secretary at the Watervliet Arsenal near Troy. She moved into a small house with family friends Kitty and John McTigue. Her new job meant new friends and challenges. Mary found time to take evening classes at Sienna College where John was completing his bachelor's degree.

While the O'Hara's were pleased for Mary in her new surroundings, the impact of her absence at home was heavy. The family was now down to just Kate and Bill. There was a sharp decrease in telephone calls and social activity. Although Bill missed Mary at evening dishwashing time (who wouldn't?), he most of all missed their conversations. Mary was simply someone to talk with about things that seemed important.

It was Mary who suggested Bill study a non-technical program in high school. That left College Prep or Commercial. Bill chose the Commercial course and this turned out to be a good choice. It was a base that helped him later on, both in the Army and in business.

Speaking of business matters, Bill's grocery and meat shopping trips had become much more organized and professional. The grocers and butchers all knew him. Because of time restraints, he would place the meat orders first and then select groceries. This was an every other day activity. Kate described her needs as far as roasts, pork or beef, chops, steak, veal and bacon and then wrote out her grocery list. Bill's arms seemed to grow longer carrying all the packages home. After all, he was now too old to pull a wagon.

Meanwhile, new faces appeared around the dinner table. One was Ed Farrell from Scranton, Pennsylvania. He transferred to Utica with the F.W. Woolworth Company. This worked out fine for Bill resulting in a part-time job at Christmastime.

Also new were Howard Ramsey and Jim Duggan, toolmakers from Whitensville, Massachusetts who were employed at Savage Arms. On their first day of work, they asked John Marriott, a tool crib clerk, about a place to live. He gave them Kate's name and address. John had been taking his dinners at Kate's and described the quality of her meals. Both moved in and proved to be delightful additions.

About this time, Tim Smiddy's brother died in Boston and left Tim the sum of $25,000.00. That was an astronomical sum in those days. Tim had never had two nickels to his name. Suddenly, he would disappear for days at a time. He traveled to Boston several times on the NYCRR. On one return trip, he got lost and ended up in Buffalo.

Tim was very popular in the taverns on South Street where he treated everyone. Kate talked Tim into visiting the Quinn and Ryan Funeral Home and he signed a contract - just in case. For the amount of $250.00, arrangements would be taken care of if something should happen. Some twenty-two years later, at the age of 87 when Tim passed away, this contract was honored to the letter including transportation and burial in Boston.

It didn't take long before his brother's estate money was all gone. Tim was once again back to his old quiet self except for a splurge on payday. Kate and the others urged him to stay on the straight and narrow. Sometimes these discussions ended in arguments.

Following one such disagreement, Tim purchased a framed picture of birds on a tree branch titled "Dogwood Time". He intended this as a gift for the disturbance he had created. Kate accepted the picture but scolded him for his earlier conduct. One word led to another until Kate took Tim by the arm. Out the kitchen door and onto the porch he went. She locked the door behind him. Tim walked around to the front door, used his key to enter the house and removed the bird picture.

He was then absent for a few days but finally returned broke and sober with the picture in tow, ready to make peace with everyone in the house. When sober, Tim was like a church mouse but when not sober, he had a 180-degree change in personality.

Kate maintained her busy schedule and, as always, her baking, cooking and meals were second to none. She continued to attend the Friday night K of C bingo. She also attended "Bank Night" at a nearby theater with Helen. Up everyday at 5 AM, Kate worked into the evening but would take about twenty minutes in the afternoon to rest or read. She liked the weekly issue of Street & Smith's "Love Stories", a fifteen-cent publication, very mild in comparison to later standards. She sat in her favorite chair by the sunlit window enjoying her twenty minutes.

Recent arrival Jim Duggan was about 6 foot, 4 inches and had played high school sports before becoming a tool-maker. Some of his former high school classmates had gone on to Holy Cross and to Boston College. Jim was excited to learn that some of his friends on the Holy Cross team would be staying at the Hotel Utica overnight before playing Syracuse University the next day at Archebald Stadium. After talking it over with Kate, Jim invited the coach and about eighteen players to Friday night dinner. Bill made a special trip to Jones' Fish Market on Pearl Street. Kate hurried the regular diners through by 5:30. She then prepared for the football players who arrived about 6:30.

In the meantime, word spread through the neighborhood and several young fans were found to be looking in the dining room windows. It took both the dining room and living room to accommodate everyone. The guests sat down to a dinner of fish, potatoes, vegetables, rolls and apple pie with tea or coffee. They were most appreciative. One of the players was Joe Boratyn, a halfback and good friend of Duggan's. It was a great event, except for the dishes!

Mary arrived home for the weekend. She and Jim attended the game in Syracuse. Holy Cross almost won.

One day that fall, Bill went hunting with Bill O'Connor for partridge and pheasants. The early morning hunt in woods near Holland Patent was the greatest. O'Connor usually bagged a couple of birds, assisted by his hunting dog, Duke. While O'Connor was intent on getting birds, Bill was satisfied just to get out into the open country with his single barrel shotgun. Catherine and Bill had given him this engraved Savage handmade gun on his 16th birthday.

One Sunday afternoon in December, Bill went home for a short work break from his job at the Stanley Theater. He was pleased to find Phil Graziano who was on leave from the Navy. Phil was a friend from his Bleecker Street days. He was to become a Chief Petty Officer. The date was December 7, 1941 and the country had just learned of the attack on Pearl Harbor. This was the subject of conversation everywhere that afternoon. Phil was scheduled to return to duty the next week. Kate made sure he had his favorite treat: her apple pie.

Over the next few historic days, everyone listened to the radio and kept up on developments via the newspapers. Headlines carried the message that war was declared by the United States along with developments in the Pacific areas.

Bob Sweeney, formerly employed at Reichardt's Drug Store, was killed on the USS Arizona. A great sadness spread throughout the neighborhood as Bob had been a friendly, well-liked young man.

During the Christmas season, the Utica Post Office opened a number of temporary part-time jobs. Bill landed one of these assignments which involved clerical work and time cards. His friends were all hauling mailbags or loading trucks. Bill's supervisor was a Mr. Murphy, who couldn't have been more helpful. His son played clarinet in the UFA band with Bill. It was a great experience working and meeting new people with new work routines.

The post office lunch break of thirty minutes allowed time to dash across the street to Donalty's Tavern. This was the gathering place. Beer flowed freely and steadily. But for Bill, it was Coca-Cola or coffee. A large ham sandwich cost fifteen-cents. On the bar were plates of cheese and crackers, free of charge. No women were allowed inside. A beer and sandwich or plate of food was often carried out to a little woman who remained in a car parked nearby. At lunchtime, one could pick up rumors and key data about what was happening at work. Later, the tavern became known as Donalty and Callahan's.

Sometimes, the postmaster, Charlie Donnelly, walked by and might stop and ask your name or that of your parents and perhaps where you lived. The group leader was a Mr. Pacilio. In all, it was an extremely busy place in the days before FedEX, UPS and other firms. The cost of first-class postage was 3-cents. Mail was delivered twice daily. Sunday was a workday and Bill would attend 7 AM Mass at nearby St. John's. Leaving a few minutes early, he dashed to work at 7:30, having to go only two blocks distance. Part-time work had to fit in between home and school schedules with school getting top priority. The income helped at home and for the holidays. Most of Bill's friends had part-time work of some type. There were manpower shortages due to volunteers for service and the draft.

The winter months of early 1942 began to see many changes due to the conflict. The draft began to affect people nearby and volunteers were joining the Army, Navy, Marines, Army Air Force or Coast Guard. Some UFA students in third and fourth year were leaving school to join. Ration books were new to everyone. Kate decided to collect ration books from all the boarders and use them to make purchases of meats and food. She next centered her purchases to two dealers, one of whom delivered. Sugar and butter were two of the items that became scarce. Although Kate did not own a car, gasoline rationing was now underway.

Everyone became very patriotic and wanted to help in the war effort. The NYCRR was hauling great amounts of war-produced goods. The Utica Freight terminal was very short of help. Joe Roddy told Bill about openings. Bill cut back his Stanley schedule and started working Saturdays and Sundays from 7 AM to 6 PM. His rate was $ .66 an hour on Saturday; time and a half on Sunday or $ .99 per hour. The weekend pay amounted to some $16.50 before Social Security. This income was helpful to the budget.

His job involved the use of a two-wheel cart to transfer shipments from one freight car to another. Utica was a "breakdown" point. The work force at the Freight Yard was very lively to say the least. Any and every type of person worked there, some full-time, others part-time. Most were hard workers. Everyone brought a lunch bag and coffee bottle marked with his name. No one ever stole a lunch. It just did not happen. There were no lunchrooms, vending machines or diners. Kate packed a few sandwiches, cookies and a thermos of coffee for Bill. The work group always had time for jokes or pranks, all well intended. This was all out-of-doors work with no breaks except for lunch.

Kate found that prices had increased for food items due to shortages. It was necessary to raise board and room to $10 per week, still a bargain.

Many an afternoon, Kate's lady friends stopped for a cup of tea. They would compare recipes, exchange news and talk over old times. Their visits were short since Kate would need to get preparations underway for dinner at 5:30.

Two late afternoon visitors were Tom Neary and Patty McMyler. They rarely came by together. Each was very animated and always had a story or two. Naturally, Kate would provide a water glass full of refreshment that was invariably met with acceptance, especially on a freezing cold day. She was happy to see them and never hurried them out the door. Actually, after the glass of refreshment, Neary and McMyler were glad to leave the hot kitchen in search of some fresh air. Bill learned not to shake hands with either man since they had bear-like grips. On more than one occasion, Kate sent a pie along home with her visitors.

To the delight of everyone at the boarding house, Mary transferred from the Watervliet Arsenal to Savage Arms and moved back home. The family was again up to a count of three. At the same time, Mary's friends at Savage Arms and members of the family began to call while the social level of activities grew higher and higher on the chart. Weekend dances and office parties were the thing. A small band or combo provided music and dancing would go from 8 PM until midnight. The Twin Ponds Country Club was a favorite location. Incidentally, Bill hired out to run the coatroom and for this would receive

$.50 an evening. The only problem was staying awake until midnight.

In spite of school schedules, music, part-time work and helping at home (sure glad Mary was back), Bill found time for his own social activities. But sometimes, Peggy, Betty or the new girl in study hall simply couldn't find the time for a date. Perhaps there was a message there.

At the end of March, Bill "retired" from the NYCRR Freight Terminal and went out for the UFA track team. Practice began indoors at the Hughes School gym and moved outside in early April. Track events were all new to Bill. He looked over his options especially the events with practice at Murnane Field.

The 100-yard dash looked too fast and, besides, there were hurdles in some of the races. The mile run required four times around the quarter-mile oval. That seemed like too much. The shot put, high jump and pole vault did not appeal to him. Nor did the half-mile run. Bill settled on the quarter-mile, or 440-yard run. Just once around the oval track.

Practice was held after school and on Saturday mornings. It was a great team under Coach Jared Howland. Competition at meets included schools such as Proctor, Nott Terrace, and Mount Pleasant from Schenectady along with Rome Free Academy, Binghamton North and others. Team members met quite a few fine runners who made it exciting to compete.

One Tuesday in May Bill took a bad fall on the cinder track that opened up the front and back of his left knee. For the first time, he took the bus home. Kate was not happy. Mary took him to the doctor who patched him up but couldn't remove all the cinders. Bill's knee took some time to heal and so the season ended early for him. But not before he had participated successfully in a few meets.

It was just as well that his track career ended short since his school schedule was so full. He was now playing trumpet in both band and school orchestra. Through music, he made many new friends.

Under the direction of Lincoln Holroyd, the band and orchestra earned a fine reputation for quality performances both on stage and as a marching unit. Music selections for the band included stirring marches like "The Stars and Stripes Forever" by John Phillip Sousa and operettas like "The Student Prince" by Sigmund Rothbard. The band performed at all UFA football games under great leadership by drum major Bill Garner.

At the end of the school term in June 1942, Bill applied for summer work with the NYCRR Signal Department. He was hired as a helper. 1942 turned out to be a summer of high adventure. The work location was in the heart of the Utica rail yards. At that time, in addition to a maze of yard tracks and switches, the railroad maintained four main line tracks, two east and two west for passenger and freight trains. Each train was pulled by huge steam driven locomotives. Rail traffic was very heavy day and night, partly due to the war effort.

The Signal Department was installing new electrical switchboxes as work took place right on the main lines. Extreme safety measures were observed. The work crew stood well aside while a passenger train flew by or a slower freight train pulled a huge steam monster locomotive by. Flat cars were loaded with trucks, jeeps, tanks and other war material, all headed for the East Coast. Troop trains would also pass and everyone waved.

One of the mechanics, Guard Troy, adopted Bill to be sure he followed safety precautions. They became good friends. It turned out to be an extremely hot, tough summer and early on, Bill switched from hot coffee to water in his thermos. Kate packed a full bag of sandwiches, fruit and cookies each day. What one took was all he had to eat. However, some of the group seemed to know where the nearest tavern or restaurant was located and bought lunch along with some liquid thirst-quencher as well. Lionel Batty, "Tiny" Williams and George Neimeyer were a part of the work crew in the Signal Department.

Some mornings, the crew would load up a small, flat rail car trailer with tools, supplies and equipment. This was hitched to a rail motorcar that had bench seats. It was then off on the westbound passenger track heading for Canastota some 35 miles distance. The project required a refurbished signal tower and some electrical switch boxes. The work was to last three weeks.

Riding the motorcar up the track in the early morning, foreman Jack Shaw consulted his pocket watch frequently. At a signal, he ordered the car to stop and be lifted off the main line track. All stood to one side. Soon, a westbound passenger or mail train would rush by at about 70 miles per hour. Then it was back with the little cars on the track traveling westward. The crew had complete confidence in Mr. Shaw and his pocket watch. However, Bill would steal a look over his shoulder now and then and noticed others doing the same. It never hurt to be sure when it came to train schedules.

At the job site, the Signal crew worked alongside a group of track workers. The track gang moved the rails into place, in line with the location of new switches. They were a hard working, friendly crew.

One of the track gang ringleaders was Tony. He brought an enormous lunch each day. His wife would slit a full loaf of Italian bread and fill it with meat, onions, peppers, tomatoes and cheese. One day Tony complained of an upset stomach. He said that he had eaten too much of the "big-eye chick". When questioned, he claimed that he had eaten an owl for supper the night before. It did not agree with him. Bill was never sure about this story, but was impressed with Tony's consumption of red hot peppers that had no apparent affect on him.

Because it took so long to travel to the job site and due to rain on several days, the superintendent, Bill Shipman, got permission for the work crew to ride on the 7:10 AM passenger train. They would be confined to the smoker car and overalls could not be worn on the train. This was to be Bill's first ride on a train. He wore a clean outfit with his hair slicked down. He found a seat, placed his overalls and lunch bag on the overhead rack and enjoyed his first train experience. Next to him was a heavy-set, bald man to whom Bill wished a "Good morning." This was ignored while the man lost himself in a newspaper.

On the trip, the train bounced around somewhat and Bill's fellow passenger began to scratch his head, appearing to be brushing away some annoyance. He looked up, trying to find the source of this itching. Suddenly, near Canastota, Bill stood up, removed his lunch and overalls from the overhead rack and stood by the exit door. He came to the conclusion that it was the sand sifting out of his overall cuffs that was annoying the man. On the way home, Bill placed his overalls under his seat.

For all the pulling wire, shoveling sand, running for

tools and riding the trains, Bill brought home a grand total of $36.42, paid in cash every two weeks. This, minus
about $5.00, was turned over to Kate for operation of the
home. This more than took care of Bill's social expendi-
tures including dates, movies, sodas, bus fare and a
ballgame or two. A new Arrow shirt sold for $2.15; an
Arrow tie, $ .49.

One day Bill saw a neat looking 1932 Ford convertible for sale at the Gulf station near New Hartford. The
price was $15.00. Even after his most effective sales pitch
to Kate, her answer was a firm "No". She was no doubt
right, as usual, but the car certainly looked appealing.

After working a hot summer day, the Signal crew
walked over to Donalty's, only a block from the railroad
station. Once there, no one spoke until after at least one
cold draught beer or two. Bill drank Coke. Upon arriving
home, he found supper ready. Mary joined him and asked
all about his day in the railroad world and then told him
about the latest at Savage Arms. On more than one night,
Bill was ready to call it quits at 9:00, 17 years of age not-
withstanding.

The world news continued to overshadow everyone's
life. In June, the battle of Midway resulted in a Naval victory over the Japanese. On August 7, the 1st Marine Division stormed ashore at Tulagi and at Guadalcanal in the
British Solomon Islands, South Pacific. Tulagi was taken
quickly but the battle on Guadalcanal lasted into 1943.

Newspaper headlines of June 22, 1942 reported that
General Rommel captured Tobruk and that Japanese
troops invaded Kiska in the Aleutian Islands.

EIGHT

KATE WAS OPERATING a nearly full boarding house. Earlier in the year, Mary's engagement to Jim Duggan had been announced. The date was set for September 26 and preparations started during the summer months.

Nearby Rome Army Air Base was in full swing. Three newcomers living at Kate's were John (Jack) Rowane, Frank Cieva and Sidney Jacobs. Jacobs drove a 1934 Chevrolet Coupe in perfect mechanical condition. All were graduates of the Casey Jones School of Aeronautics and were employed as mechanics at the Base. Jacobs could drive the Chevrolet two hundred and forty miles to New York City in five hours flat. This was prior to expressways and the New York State Thruway.

Kate treated these young men like members of her own family. Their work shifts started at 6:00 PM. They slept part of the afternoon and were slow to get up and get moving. One day, with dinner getting cold on the table, Kate marched upstairs to their bedrooms with a kettle of scalding water and began to pour it on each of them, still in bed. That solved the problem. They leaped out of bed in their underwear. Jack, Frank and Sid became very good friends with Kate and Bill. The boarding house for them was a home away from home. If they became ill, Kate got them better in no time.

The summer flew by and suddenly it was the last week in August. Bill left his summer job with the NYCRR a few days early and reported for UFA football practice (a big mistake) at Murnane Field. Having been influenced by the Holy Cross football team's visit, he decided to try out upon entering his Senior year (second mistake). He was issued a uniform and became left guard on the second string. Second string's job was to play against the first string varsity players four nights a week. On Saturday at the game, Bill and the secondary warmed the bench. On occasion, a substitute would be sent in.

The season was going only fair and at one practice, Coach Ken Edkins chastised the players for lack of aggressiveness. He really chewed. Bill got the message and on the very next play, sailed over his opposing guard and slammed helmet first into the halfback, one Mr. Vialas. This resulted in a gush of blood and a called time-out.

The coach demanded, "Who did this? Who caused this?" Everyone looked around. Bill raised his hand.

Coach Edkins asked, "What's your name?"

The weak reply came back, "O'Hara."

The coach then bellowed out in a very loud voice, "This is great! It's what I want to see more of on this field! More blood and more often, just like O'Hara caused!"

Practice resumed. Another mistake. Bill knew he was in for it even before the next play during which eight or nine players piled on him. He had to be helped up, could not catch a breath and time was called. The coach told him to take the rest of the practice off and he again took the bus home.

That night he was visited by Dr. Jim Douglas who determined Bill had no broken ribs but a torn cartilage. As Dr. Douglas began to wrap a wide adhesive tape around the chest area, he told Bill about his days on the UFA football team when he also played left guard. It became uncomfortable to take a deep breath, cough or sneeze. The tape remained in place for about two weeks. Going up stairs became a challenge. It was the end of a promising football career. The question remained, just how did those Holy Cross guys do it? The real fun came when the doctor tore the tape off and pronounced Bill back to normal, less any hairs on his chest.

Suddenly it was September 26, Mary and Jim's wedding day. There was great activity at the house. Kate's sisters, Mariah, Maggie and Rose were on hand for the day. As at all weddings, there seemed to be a large number of people rushing about doing nothing important but all of which seemed important at the time. Gifts were delivered, cars were double-parked out front, and flowers arrived…lots of confusion.

Finally, it was time for the church. The wedding took place at 11:00 AM at St. John's Church. Catherine was the matron of honor and Joe Boratyn was best man. The ushers were Mary's brothers Martin, James, John and Bill, along with Bill Roberts, a friend. The ceremony went very well and Mary looked elegant. Kate looked wonderful as the mother of the bride. Jim Duggan carried on well and if he was nervous, he did not show it.

The church was filled with friends, relatives, neighbors and a large gathering of Mary and Jim's co-workers from Savage Arms. Following the ceremony, the bridal party traveled to the Yahnundasis Golf Club for brunch and pictures. Later, everyone returned to the boarding house for an afternoon reception.

It was impossible to fit one more person in the house, on the steps, in the yard or anywhere nearby. Laughter and conversation filled the house. Happiness was complete. Presents lined the dining room table. No one left early. The refreshments and the food were plentiful. A considerable number of Irish "old timers" gathered in the kitchen to swap stories and actively participate in liquid refreshments. It was probably the last really big Irish gathering of family and friends since the ranks had already thinned somewhat. The only thing missing was the fiddler and some dancing.

The afternoon went by all too quickly. At 4:30, suitcases and some of the gifts were loaded into Mary and Jim's 1939 Dodge convertible. Everyone went out to the street to see them off. They both looked radiant. It was a beautiful, sunny fall afternoon. The last anyone saw of them was a wave, as they pulled down the street and off to West Newton, Massachusetts and onto their new life together.

Kate and Bill felt Mary's absence. Although they were very happy for her, once more the family was down to just the two of them.

A couple of weeks went by and Kate and Bill received their first letter from Mary and Jim, telling about their new place and activities. Jim was employed as a toolmaker at the A.H. Nichols Company and liked his job. They sounded truly happy. Thanksgiving came and went but they were unable to get home.

NINE

BILL HAD BEEN following the Holy Cross football results all season. The team had done quite well overall. However, they were to play undefeated Boston College on Saturday, November 28. No one was willing to wager on Holy Cross.

Talk about a miracle. It was an upset, a total rout. Holy Cross won 55-6! Joe Boratyn played halfback for Holy Cross. All radio broadcasts carried the score and the game made most major newspapers in the northeast.

Boston College fans had planned a celebration that evening in downtown Boston at a popular nightclub known as the Cocoanut Grove. The BC fans ended up selling their reservations to the Holy Cross crowd for that evening.

Sunday morning, November 29, Kate and Bill attended 7 AM Mass at St. John's Church. Afterward, at breakfast, the local Observer Dispatch newspaper was on the table with a headline concerning Boston's Cocoanut Grove fire.

"I hope Mary and Jim were not at that place," Bill said to Kate.

Kate replied, "Now why would they be there?"

At about 11 AM, Bill went shopping for groceries and meat up on South Street. He was away about a half-hour, just starting back with loaded bags of food. Frank Cieva hurried up to him saying, "Bill, you should hurry right home. Your mother needs you." Frank offered to carry the groceries.

Bill asked, "What's wrong? What happened?" Again, Frank urged him to get along.

As he approached the house, Bill saw Jack and Sidney at the door waiting for him. Neither said anything. Hurrying into the dining room, Bill saw Kate sitting in her chair by the window, tears running down her face. "What happened?"

Kate was unable to speak. She was white. Bill took a yellow sheet of paper from her hand. It was a telegram reading:

MARY O'HARA DUGGAN DIED AT MASS GENERAL HOSPITAL NOVEMBER 29. PLEASE ADVISE.

Bill handed the telegram to Jack Rowane. He talked with Kate and said he would call Catherine and the rest of the family.

The shock was so devastating that Bill had great difficulty making the members of the family believe him. He couldn't believe it himself. He read them the telegram. Soon they began to arrive. Some were visibly upset. Others were in shock. Jim and Mary had indeed attended the Cocoanut Grove. Joe Boratyn was with them and was also lost in the fire.

Arrangements were made that afternoon with Quinn and Ryan Funeral Home. Kate and Bill were devastated but had to keep going. They learned that Jim Duggan had been severely burned and was at the hospital in Boston. He was allowed no visitors. He did not recover sufficiently to allow a trip to the boarding house until the following April.

Mary's body arrived by train the next day. She was to be buried in her wedding dress. The casket was closed. The wake was held at home.

It was with great sadness that the same people who attended her wedding just eight weeks earlier were now in attendance to pay their respects. Many familiar faces attended the funeral Mass at St. John's Church. Just about the entire Savage Arms office was there. Everyone seemed to be looking out through tears, lost in their own thoughts. The question was simply: how could this be?

The weather that day seemed to reflect everyone's feelings. It was overcast, bitter cold with a high wind and swirling snow. Mary was laid to rest at Mount Olivet Cemetery, next to her father.

Over the next few days, it was simply a case of trying to get by. All the boarders ate out. Jack Rowane, Frank Cieva and Sid Jacobs were a great help. They took on some of the routine tasks around the house. Neighbors, friends and relatives were most helpful. Many sent in food and baked goods. Some offered financial assistance which Kate graciously declined. It was such a terribly unreal period of time for all. The following week, Bill returned to school but was excused from band and orchestra on a temporary basis.

About ten days following the burial, a box arrived from Massachusetts General Hospital. In it were Mary's clothing items and what personal effects she had at the time. This rekindled great sadness for all and was again almost too much to bear.

At a later time, the O'Hara's learned what took place at the Cocoanut Grove on that terrible night. According to newspaper and other reports, a flash fire broke out and spread rapidly through the many decorations, giving off toxic-like vapors. The fumes quickly spread and all the lights went out. The exit doors jammed with people and no one could get out. Other doors had been nailed shut. Some 490 people died and some 166 were hospitalized, many for quite a long period.

December moved along and the family turned away from Christmas decorations. Suddenly, it was a few days before Christmas.

Bill spoke to Kate. "We should have a little tree with Mary's strings of blue lights. She would have liked that."

Kate was not in total agreement. Bill went out and bought a modest tree. He placed the Christmas light strings - all blue - on the tree with no other decorations. It looked quite solemn in the living room. Jack, Frank and Sid, along with others, came and looked it over. It helped everyone get through Christmas as tears flowed from both family members and friends alike.

That little tree with blue lights seemed to take on a special meaning for all in the boarding house that Christmas.

TEN

THE HOLIDAYS WENT by quickly. Bill went back to the NYCRR Freight Terminal for weekend work. This left his weeknights free to help Kate.

During this time, war news continued to hold everyone's attention. The Selective Service System was pulling more and more young men into active duty. Several of Bill's friends left school to enlist. The Navy and Marines were the most attractive branches along with the Army Air Corps. On February 4, 1943 Bill turned 18 years old and registered for the draft. Since he was a high school senior with passing grades, he was deferred until the end of the school term. Bill's friend, Bob Miller, had left for the Marines. Bob's older brother, Joe, had become a Marine earlier.

Senior year, especially the last five months, left no time for much other than study and schoolwork. Homework assignments were heavy and it seemed that everything was a straight rush downhill to high school completion. That was the case up to the last week of March. Bill had felt some pain in his right side but thought he pulled a muscle at the Freight House. The pain persisted and a visit was made to Dr. Douglas who determined a problem with his appendix. Surgery was the last thing he felt he needed at the time.

Dr. Douglas assured Bill that an appendix removal was very common. There should be no concern. So, on April 1 at St. Elizabeth Hospital, out came the appendix. Dr. Douglas was well known for his brevity and tight schedules. He lived up to his reputation with a six-minute operation and a 3/4 inch incision. Dr. Douglas took a keen interest in Bill and came by everyday.

Kate made a visit. Catherine was in town and one night Helen visited too. That was the night the track team came by. Clarence Bass, Ted Grimes, Harold Moore, Fred Williams and other members of the team checked in on Bill. Helen was leaving for the Stanley Theater Bank Night and was offered a ride down Genesee Street with Bill's friends. She accepted. Unknown to her, they drove a 1934 Ford four-door but the doors were tied closed with ropes. Bill nearly split his sides knowing the condition of the car. At the least, they were sincere.

Interestingly, no invoice arrived from Dr. Douglas. Kate called and his secretary, Mrs. Davis, told her not to wait for one. The doctor normally charged $35.00 for an appendix removal. Dr. Douglas never even asked for an apple pie as his father had done years before.

It was a coincidence but another senior, Walter Sheridan, also required an appendix operation. He was at the same hospital and operated on by Dr. Douglas within a day of Bill. Walt had been the UFA quarterback.

Homework assignments were sent to Bill and Walt. Olive Smith, History "C" teacher, pushed both boys to complete their assignments and to get back to class. Just one week following surgery, Miss Smith was on the telephone requesting a date to return to school. It was through her efforts and interest that both young men were able to keep up and make up lost time.

In the meantime, Kate was trying to fatten Bill up with her best baking and cooking efforts. Her homemade biscuits, dumplings, spare ribs, brown gravy and always mashed potatoes followed by apple pie or, in early June, strawberry shortcake with real whipped cream, could never be forgotten. In fact, no one ever heard of a complaint on her meals.

That springtime, a blessed event took place for Catherine and Bill O'Connor. A little girl arrived and was named Kathleen.

Throughout high school classes, band, orchestra and track, Bill made many life-long friends. In Homeroom 120, Miss Mabel Onderdonk was the teacher. She taught Algebra. The blackboards were filled with equations. She and Bill got on fine. However, being a few minutes late each day did not sit well with her. Just prior to graduation, she called Bill aside and said, "Mr. O'Hara, you have the record for coming in late more than any other student in my 30 years of teaching." Bill replied, "I really liked Homeroom 120 and insofar as lateness, you need have no concern after June 23rd, Graduation Day." Bill told her how much he appreciated her as his homeroom teacher.

During the four years in Homeroom 120, Louis Novak sat directly in front of Bill. Maria Whelley sat one seat behind and Clarence Hoagland sat to the left. Bill Price had a seat over to the right. Lou Novak worked a late shift at the NYCRR Freight Yards logging boxcar numbers for the make up of trains. He worked from around 5 PM to 1 AM and, in addition, carried a heavy subject load including Physics, Trigonometry, History C and labs. Lou rarely studied. He would read his lessons once and that was it. On some mornings in Homeroom 120 when the bell rang to leave for their first class, Bill would poke Lou to be sure he was awake. Then it was up and off to a full day of classes.

Bill Price was a friendly, energetic young man, taking a college prep program. Following graduation, he would become a member of the Navy and later join the Maryknoll Missionaries, serving about 40 years in Guatemala.

On Friday mornings while attendance was taken in homerooms, about a dozen band members would parade through the halls playing marches such as "On Wisconsin" or "Victory March" to remind students of the football or basketball game that weekend. This group was mostly brass: trumpets, trombones, drums, cymbals and a few clarinets. The floors were tile. The noise level easily exceeded 90 decibels. They got everyone's attention.

During regular band and orchestra sessions, it was a different story. Fine performances were accomplished. Several members were outstanding including Bob Jones on trombone and Don Fague on trumpet. One trumpet player, Fred Gregory, went on to play in the Navy Band. Great musical arrangements acquainted Bill with some fine works. Music from "The Student Prince" by Sigmund Romberg, marches by John Philip Sousa and others were presented. In orchestra, Ray Caine and Bill played trumpet. Both band and orchestra presented concerts that were always well attended. In addition, the band performed at all home football games.

At the start of the senior year, a new subject, Junior Aviation, was offered as an extra. Some twenty-two students signed up with Bill including Don Irion and Lou Novak. At that time during the war, they felt this course might come in handy. Three classes per week were held including lab time. A yellow Piper Cub was delivered and set up in the auto mechanics auditorium. The instructor, Robert Stewart, taught engine upkeep, fabric repair, meteorology and ground support. While everyone enjoyed the subject immensely, they were unable to get the engine started.

They had taken it all apart and assumed that it had not been put back together correctly. Everyone tried the propeller to turn it over, but to no avail. Safety rules required one person to be in the airplane when the prop was spun. This was in order to reduce power. The wheels were securely blocked to the shop floor.

It was the first morning of Regents week in June and the school building was as quiet as a cemetery. Someone went up to give the prop one last good spin. Although no one was in the airplane, the throttle had been left wide-open. The engine sputtered, coughed and sprang to life with a roar that could be heard for a city block. The plane strained at the blocks. All room drawings, blueprints and loose papers went flying in every direction. Bob Stewart dashed to the open door and shut the power off. There was shocked silence and then a class cheer but only briefly since the school principal and several very upset teachers arrived. The Junior Aviation class wasn't too worried about suspension; it was their last week at UFA. No one had been injured but the roar of that Piper Cub inside the building remained with the Class of '43 and the school for a long time. It was a great way to wind up the year.

Everyone qualified for graduation but not without a

great deal of study, midnight oil-burning, nail-biting and praying. Finally, on Wednesday, June 23, graduation ceremonies were held at the Stanley Theater. It was a beautiful, sunny summer day and everyone looked his or her best. The Senior Ball took place that evening at the Hotel Utica. Bill and his date enjoyed a great evening of dancing and chatting with classmates. However, there was a distinct feeling of finality about this affair. A large percent of the young men attending had reporting dates for the service. Only a few were heading to college.

Bill had been served notice to report for a physical exam on June 21 at the Steuben Street Armory. This took from 8:00 AM until 3:00 PM. He passed his physical, was sworn into the Army and was given a departure date of July 5.

Upon arriving home, he explained these developments to Kate, who said nothing as tears flowed down her face. She busied herself at the stove where Bill's lunch had been kept warm. They sat at the kitchen table and talked things over. Bill was more concerned with Kate's welfare than he was about leaving for the Army. He made several suggestions like getting a young man to do her shopping.

He explained his plan to sign up for a dependent's allotment and Kate would receive a check each month for $37.50. Out of his $50.00 per month, he would have deducted $22.00. The government would make up the difference. This would pay the monthly mortgage on the boarding house, solving a serious problem. In addition, for the cost of $6.40, Bill would take out a $10,000.00 National Service Life Insurance policy with Kate as the beneficiary.

After listening, Kate said quietly, "I'd simply rather have you at home."

That evening, Bill visited Catherine and reviewed all

dates and details with her. This meant that the family would now be down to only Kate at home. Catherine promised to keep an eye on things as best she could.

The next two weeks flew by like the snap of his fingers. Bill visited his friends, kept dentist and optometrist appointments, called Dr. Douglas and sorted out his few belongings. He turned his shotgun over to Bill O'Connor for safekeeping. He spent a little time visiting St. John' Church.

On the morning of July 5, Kate had a nice breakfast ready. All of the boarders were on hand, but most skipped breakfast at the house that day. Bill packed a small gym bag. He did not own a suitcase. One of the boarders, Fred Freeman, shook Bill's hand and pressed a $20.00 bill into his palm. Kate too gave him a $20.00 bill - just for emergencies. It was a beautiful summer day for a trip.

Bill asked Kate to say goodbye at home but she planned to go to the railroad station, riding along with Catherine and Bill.

Bill was part of a large group leaving that day. They were required to report to City Hall. Looking around the room, Bill knew many on a first name basis. After roll call, they marched in a loose formation down Genesee Street to the NYCRR station. To his astonishment, Bill found several thousand people on hand to see the recruits off to training. Friends, neighbors, several teachers and all of his family were there. The holiday brought everyone out. The station, sidewalks, platform and surrounding areas were jammed. It was elbow to elbow with everyone talking at once.

Most seemed quite nervous and a bit apprehensive. Finally, it was time to shake hands with the guys and give a quick kiss to Catherine and Helen. Bill held on to Kate

James B. O'Hara
1904

Catherine Neary O'Hara
1904

William M. O'Hara
1943

Mary J. O'Hara
June 1942

Sunday visitors and card players all. Jim O'Hara 2nd left, Kate far right

*A summer Sunday with the McTige's of Troy, NY.
Young Bill in foreground. Circa 1929*

*Kate and Jim O'Hara
Circa 1929*

Kate and Irish friend, 1941

*Mary O'Hara Duggan and sister, Catherine
E. O'Connor, Sept. 1942*

the longest, gave her a peck on the cheek, promised to write on a regular basis and call when he got to his first permanent location. Kate had no reply. Her tears said it all.

Suddenly, it was time to hop on the train. The "All Aboard!" was called out three times. In just a moment, the sea of faces of family and friends was left behind and the countryside went rushing by the window. The train moved swiftly down the Mohawk Valley in the bright summer sunshine.

Lou Novak sat with Bill. How ironic, after four years in Homeroom 120 at only one seat apart, there they were together again, en route to a great adventure. No one spoke for some 30 to 40 minutes. Lost in thought, they tried to adjust to an emotional transition from the departure scene. Each had his own private thoughts to sort out concerning family, girlfriends and plans.

Suddenly, it was noon and the recruits were directed to the Pullman dining car for their first meal on the Army. Other members of the just-graduated UFA class joined Lou and Bill. Over lunch, they began speculating over what opportunities would be available to them. Some planned to take tests for the Army Air Force.

Lou told Bill, "I'm going to volunteer for the paratroops and this will pay me $50.00 a month on top of the regular $50.00." Bill urged Lou to go slow on volunteering and instead simply see what might materialize as far as assignments. Lou, however, had his mind set and did volunteer. He was sent to Fort Benning, Georgia. His entry was poorly timed since all the paratroop quotas were filled. He was instead assigned to the Field Artillery.

Bill never saw Lou Novak again. Later in 1944, Bill received a news clip from home that announced Lou had been killed in action in Italy. He had been a Forward Observer with the Field Artillery. He was just 19. A close friend lost.

The men changed trains in New York City and continued on to Camp Upton, Long Island. The last half-hour travel was by bus to the main gate, arriving about 7:30 PM. Everyone was lined up and separated into two groups: white and non-white. This was prior to service integration. Bill's black high school friends went in one direction and the rest of the group went through a cafeteria line. Each was assigned to a barracks. No one slept that night. All lights remained on and the talking never stopped. However, in the early morning hours, the group did drift off to some rest.

And so, on July 6 at 5:10 AM, the whistle blew for reveille. It was the beginning of a whole new day for Bill O'Hara and many like him, all starting a new way of life over the next few years.

It was a whole new day for Kate as well, and for many other parents who were to get used to their loved ones going off to the service. No one knew for how long and if and in what condition they would eventually return home.

IRISH PRIDE
AMERICAN COURAGE

Book 3

ELEVEN

ON THAT EARLY July 6 morning, the first day of Army life, a steady stream of new recruits, still dressed in civilian clothing, poured out of the Camp Upton Reception Center barracks and lined up on the company street in a loose formation. A Corporal (temporary rank) was strutting around like a two star General giving orders, blowing a whistle and letting everyone know that he definitely was in charge. No one understood his commands but tried to obey his loud demands. Following roll call, everyone went to clean up and then on to breakfast.

Back again in formation on the company street, all marched to a central building. Several types of forms were completed, some of which took place in cubicles. On one interview, the clerk noted that Bill had taken typing in high school. Then, it was a typing test on which Bill purposely did not do his best. Who wanted to be a typist in the Army?

Next, a long line formed and entered the medical building. A series of "shots" were administered for a variety of things including tetanus, typhoid and no one was sure what else. As the recruits walked down the line, names were recorded and medics on both sides of the line administered injections, some into the left arm and right arm at the same time. More than one customer keeled over. They received smelling salts and were led on their way. Quite a few appeared pale. Some took on a shade of green. Compared to the conversations in the barracks the previous night, this group was very sober and quiet.

The first real change took place in the next building. Army clothing and shoes were issued. Civilian clothing was placed into a small box, addressed and mailed home. Bill was given shoes sized 11 1/2-C. He normally wore 11-C. When this was brought to the attention of the Supply Sergeant, he was immediately told, "Wear these. You may have to carry a 100-pound bag of sand on each shoulder and your feet will need to spread." Actually, there were no 11-C shoes in stock. It took almost a year to obtain a correct fit.

More formations were called and the new soldiers, now in uniform (some too loose, some too tight, some itching) were taught to salute. Next they were taught how to do an about-face which brought about lots of laughter. Then they learned other basics. There were a good number of "sad sacks" in the ranks but then, just yesterday, they were ordinary civilians. They were required to attend movies and lectures on the prevention of social diseases. In all, it was a hectic first two days.

After dinner on Tuesday night, groups were marched to the railroad siding. Waiting there was a tired looking Long Island Express train with old-fashioned straw seats. Everyone figured this to be a real short trip with this kind of transportation. No Pullman, no dining car. The train departed at dark and the betting was underway. Would it be over 100 miles and in what direction? Card games and dice appeared to break up the monotony. Morale was high, everyone was chipper. Must be a short trip.

Few got much sleep that second night. The seats did not fold down. Some slept on the floor and kept rolling around. A few enterprising young men climbed up and slept on the overhead metal luggage carriers. In the morning they all had red lines down their backs from the bars. Finally, the call came for breakfast and they finally got to use their new mess kits.

A line formed toward the food car half way up the train. They had no idea what to expect but were not disappointed. The train was now speeding across Ohio at about 75 MPH lurching from side to side. The "dining car" was a converted baggage car. The cooks stirred enormous pans of scrambled eggs and toasted bread while working on makeshift grills. The side of the car was fully open by two double doors and a single line of rope running across the opening.

A large "GI" can full of coffee had a big block of wood floating in it to steady the coffee as the train lurched. A sign read "Beware of Slivers". Bill wondered how there could be slivers in coffee. Next, he saw the metal scoop for the coffee beating on the wood block, hence, the slivers. However, the coffee was not too bad. The slivers floated to the top and were easy to remove. Then the coffee tasted great.

That night and the following two nights were the same. The recruits crossed Indiana and were well into Illinois. Saturday morning, right after an early breakfast, the train pulled into a siding. This was not unusual since they frequently pulled over to let fast trains pass by. Then they heard, "Everyone out!" Actually, no one cared where he was. They just wanted to get away from the LIRR train. They had arrived at Camp Ellis, Illinois, a huge new training facility for Signal Corps, Combat Engineers, Quartermaster and Medical. It was located about 70 miles south of Peoria. The men were trucked to their barracks.

At the first formation on the company street, First Sergeant Joe Moreland welcomed them to Camp Ellis and to the 458th Quartermaster Company (QMC), a part of the Army Service and Supply operation. A number of the soldiers, including Bill, felt let down. They were hoping for an organization with more excitement. Technical Sergeant Gossett had them file into their barracks with double-decker bunks. The barracks held 48 men. There were new faces everywhere. Cornelius (Corney) Klass took the bottom bunk while Bill took the top. Corney was from Buffalo. Next to them were Bill Strawson from White Plains and Tom Fey from New York City. The afternoon was spent on orientation, a refresher on how to salute properly and settling in. The Company Commander, Captain Walter J. Geiser, read the Articles Of War. They met their Platoon Lieutenant, 2nd Lt. Walter Glazer and Squad Leader Sergeant McCorkel.

Early the next morning, a Sunday morning, Bill found the base chapel and attended Mass. It seemed strange to attend church and not know anyone there. Next, it was a long hike to find a pay telephone. He called Kate around 11:30 at good old Utica #4-1728. Kate was pleased with the call and glad to learn Bill was with the QMC. She had been very upset the day before. The box of clothing had arrived from Camp Upton. Kate said it reminded her of the box with Mary's belongings. She sounded a little sad.

Bill told her how great the food, living quarters and leaders were and assured her he was involved in training at Camp Ellis. Bill sent her a short letter that afternoon. Postage was only $ .03.

Sunday afternoon, the guys listened to a radio someone had brought. They couldn't find any Glenn Miller but heard a variety of "hillbilly" or "Mountain" music. Later, they learned this was known as "country music". There were a lot of preachers on the air, too.

Monday morning and the first full day of Army training arrived early. At 5:10 AM, Platoon Sergeant Gossett blew his whistle and everyone heard his "Fall out - rise and shine!" The Company lined up in Platoon formation and the individual positions were to remain for all future formations. Bill stood in the 1st Platoon, 1st Squad, sixth from the lead, right behind Bill Strawson. Corney Klass was in the 2nd Squad nearby. Roll-call preceded breakfast. Bunks were made up and shoes were shined. Their uniforms for the next 12 weeks consisted of fatigues and puttees. The latter were a wrap-around leg and ankle pant which required hooking to fasten in place. Whistles blew and off they went for a full day of close order drill. The 458th QMC Company was made up of 385 enlisted men and 5 officers.

The first four weeks required close order drill every day in all kinds of weather. Hikes, exercises, running, obstacle courses and a few lectures filled their days. One obstacle course involved swinging ropes, streams, mud pits and a wall about ten feet high. You had to run, jump up, grab the top and get over the wall. Bill tried the wall again and again. Something would pull on his right side. He explained this to Sgt. Gossett who told him to either get over the wall or go on sick call. With six to eight others, Bill went on sick call the following morning. At the base hospital, a doctor examined him and gave him a two-week reprieve on the wall climbing so his side could relax. After that, he was able to scale the wall to the cheers of Klass and Strawson.

The second four weeks included the rifle range with a good old Enfield rifle.

One Saturday afternoon, the troops were challenged with an obstacle course requiring them to crawl on the ground under barbed wire, while a 30-caliber machine gun mounted on a tripod fired an arc of blanks and some live ammunition over them. Orders issued were to keep at 18 inches or below. Some of the heavier troops barely made it. Never before did they hug the ground crawling across a field of mud. This was as realistic as training could get.

The 458th was largely men from New York State. Some 75% were from New York City. All of the sergeants and corporals were from the South, primarily Virginia and Tennessee. It soon became clear that there was no love lost between the non-commissioned officers and the troops. From day to day, nothing was ever right. Fault would be found with rifle inspection, barracks floors, uniforms and the drill routines. Actually, the troops began getting a step ahead of the cadre since they were able to anticipate much of what the non-commissioned officers planned to pick on. At times, some of the cadre were not too swift.

One thing in this new military life which came across as a shock was the common, everyday use of vulgar language. If this language was an attempt to impress others, it did not work. The Mess Sgt., Staff Sgt. Smith, also from the South, took great delight in making life miserable for the troops in a number of ways. Any soldier who might leave a scuff mark on the dining room floor was signed up for KP. Should one not eat every scrap of his meal (sometimes it was not too good), his name was taken for KP because he wasted food.

Bill served his first day on KP and made some new friends. One of these was Larry Palladino from Manhattan. KP started at 5:00 AM and continued until around 10:00 PM. Work included washing plates, cups, and flatware, floor scrubbing and, yes, even the garbage cans. After dinner, dishes were washed, rinsed and stood up to air dry. S/Sgt. Smith picked one up, claimed he saw a grease spot and ordered everything for 390 troops to be done over. Next, he directed that three bags of potatoes be pared and that the grease traps under the sinks be cleaned. That was a most disagreeable task. The KP group split the chores in half to hurry the process. Everyone was exhausted.

The potatoes were actually chopped into squares. Water was run in the sinks and the potatoes dumped in with a little water to run all night. Suddenly, one KP demanded, "Who dumped potatoes into the big sinks?" Two inches of grease scum hadn't been removed from the sinks but by now it was far too late. It was 10:45 PM. The night cook said they could leave.

By 11:00 PM the soldiers had gone through the shower and fell into their bunks. It seemed like just five minutes had passed when the 5:10 AM whistle blew. The KP's spread the word, "Do not eat the potatoes." No reason was given. The cooks could not understand why only the officers and the cadre ate potatoes that day.

One day folded into the next with a steady schedule of close order drills, rifle and full field pack included. Long hikes with full gear in all kinds of weather got everyone lean and mean. Illinois' July and August of 1943 was one of the hottest summers on record. At the end of a full day in the sun, few, if any, could eat food that was served at 5:30 PM sharp. Instead, the troops simply sat around, took a shower and at 7:00 PM, wandered to the Post Exchange (PX), and devoured a pint of ice cream with good old Coca-Cola. They bought chips or cookies because around 9:00 PM, everyone was hungry again. That would have been the time for dinner.

Klass, Strawson and O'Hara looked out for each other. In the morning before formation, each would look everything over to insure proper uniform, their knapsacks were packed correctly and rifles cleaned. One windy, rainy morning, 1st Sgt. Moreland's roll call was underway. One soldier, Private Green (not his real name) got ready to answer. He had a stuttering problem. His name was at the top of the roll call page. Green listened for the name ahead of his. Sgt. Moreland was having trouble turning his sheet. Green shouted, "Here!"

The Sgt. demanded, "Who said that?" Green raised his hand. The Sgt. said, "Next time, wait until I call your name! Now report for KP." Poor Green. Actually, he was lucky, since the others went on an all day hike in the pouring rain.

At the end of four weeks, a Saturday night pass could be requested. It lasted from 2:30 PM Saturday to 6:00 PM Sunday. Buses left camp for Peoria or Macolm. Bill traveled to Peoria with Ed Mahoney, a high school friend. An overnight at the Hotel Mayer was $2.00. Four soldiers usually shared the room and split the cost. A favorite eating spot was Bishop's Cafeteria where coffee was $ .05. Telephone calls home were made from the lobby of the Hotel Pierre Marquette.

One cold November Saturday evening, Bill and Ed walked a number of blocks looking for an inexpensive restaurant. After deductions, each had only $21.60 left for the month. They found a small Italian restaurant on a side street. It had red and white-checkered tablecloths, a great aroma of food and a friendly owner. The guys were greeted with a bottle of wine, compliments of the owner and his wife. After a fine Italian meal, they went to pay but the owner would take no money. He explained that his son was in the Army stationed in Africa. Urging them to come back again, he accepted Ed and Bill's thanks. His son's picture was on the wall.

About a month later, Ed and Bill returned to find the restaurant closed. A sign on the door read, "Closed - Death in Family - Son Killed in Action." The next morning at church, the soldiers prayed for the young man even though they didn't know his name.

The 458th had three new soldiers assigned to help with combat training. They had seen action in Africa and were very interesting. Their assignment was only about three weeks. They lectured and gave demonstrations. One night at about 2:00 AM, returning from a night on the town, their car hit a bridge post and all were killed. It seemed so ironic that, after combat overseas, they lost their lives in a car accident back home.

Letters and news from home was always the highlight of the day. Kate was a lady of few words but all was going well at the boarding house. She continued working hard to get enough food and meat through rationing in an attempt to keep everyone fed and happy. Catherine took the time to write and pass along all the news that Bill would otherwise miss out on. She sent an August news clipping about her next-door neighbor, George May. George was a gunner in the Army Air Force in Africa. His plane was shot down twice but he managed to escape, finding his way back to his unit both times.

The third week of August found the 458th at the rifle range for two weeks of intensive drill. "Ready on the right and ready on the left!" could be heard loud and clear on the range. The rifle was the Enfield. Simply from his hunting experience with Bill O'Connor, Bill had a slight advantage over those who had never handled a gun.

Trucks returned the troops in time for the 5:10 PM retreat. Every unit in the camp stood at attention in formation while the base flag was lowered. Although no one could see the ceremony at headquarters, the soldiers knew it was over from the boom of a cannon each night. Following the ceremony, the men were dismissed. They took showers and headed for the PX, too hot and exhausted to eat. The next morning at reveille, they were ordered to report to the mess hall every day at 5:30 PM where roll call was to be taken! Dinner was a must, like it or not.

The men were notified of a 25-mile hike to begin at 6:30 PM. Everyone lined up with full field pack, gas mask, rifle, helmet liner and canteen. It was a humid late August evening. The Company marched to the 12-1/2 mile point then was given a 10-minute break. It was pitch dark. Suddenly, eyes began to sting and breathing became troubled. "Tear Gas!" someone shouted. Gas masks were unhooked and put on as quickly as possible but not before everyone's eyes were tearing and smarting. The masks had a built-in odor that resembled ether. The whistle blew to "Fall In" but with masks, darkness and some confusion, there was a bit of stumbling around. Strawson lifted his mask and told Bill to grab his pack strap and away they marched for about 1/2 mile. The order was given to remove masks. A severe reprimand for poor performance in an emergency followed. Morale sank. The troops did not appreciate the timing of the gas mask drill. They marched toward camp in silence. Some had to drop out, including Corney. The weapons carrier picked up those who fell back.

Some one-half mile from the 458 barracks, a halt was called. The Signal and Engineering groups knew the troops had left on a 25-mile hike. It was around midnight. The Company formed up with lines straight across and forward. All stood tall and marched in cadence back to the barracks, just like on the drill field. Point made, all fell into bunks for the night. Corney was waiting for Bill, who felt sorry that his friend could not finish the hike.

Bill searched his footlocker for a box that had arrived that day. He shared cookies and a can of fruit cocktail with Corney, talking quietly until 2:00 AM. They were wound up too tight to sleep. Sgt. Gossett walked through the barracks, amused to note their quiet celebration of hike survival.

Army equipment lectures were presented to the troops while they sat on log seats in a semi-circle. Most talks were of no interest and heads would nod. A Corporal with a long pole walked through the group and administered a loud "Whack!" An unlucky soldier would startle and stay awake from that point on.

The outside world news in September had the Allies

invading Italy opposite Messina. Newspaper headlines on September 9, announced that Italy had surrendered.

In the Solomon Islands, US Marine and Army units extended the ground held north of Guadalcanal on Arundel and Vella Lavella while advancing on Bouganville.

In late September, a USO dance was arranged for the 458th QMC at the Camp recreational hall. The troops showered, slicked down their hair, overdid it with after-shave and polished their shoes. The ladies arrived by bus from Springfield and Peoria. As the music played, the troops could request a dance. The key was not to step on toes with their Army shoes. Bill shared a few dances. It certainly was a different evening. MP's were in attendance to maintain order. Morale improved. The following day, the dance was the talk of the barracks. Some had obtained invitations and address data.

A major event took place in the middle of October. The Company packed everything up. Footlockers went to storage, the barracks were cleaned out. The troops boarded trucks for a drive of about five hours into the country. This was to be two weeks of sleeping on the ground, hiking, living outside and roughing it up some-where along a river in Illinois. They never did find out. Strawson and Bill shared a pup tent. It turned very cold so they slipped into a nearby field and "borrowed" some hay on which to sleep. Pup tents went up just prior to a downpour. The Company stood retreat, went through the chow line with mess kits and returned to their tents to get out of the rain. The temperature took a nosedive.

The evening decision concerned how to best use their overcoats and two Army-issued blankets. They resolved to make use of all three items. The men wore their overcoats for the night and rolled up in the two blankets to keep warm.

The 5:10 AM whistle was met with creaking limbs, stiff joints and groans. Mess cups filled with red-hot coffee helped. It was like putting gasoline into the tank. Cooks served scrambled eggs, bacon and toast. Oatmeal was optional, clumps and all. Following roll-call formation, the Company marched off into a beautiful countryside and welcome sunshine. Illinois was simply great that morning. Civilians waved and were very friendly. Strawson wondered if one of them could be the farmer from whom he and Bill had appropriated the hay.

On the weekend, everyone was confined to the area. All regular food service was cancelled. The men were to eat special large chocolate bars, three per day, on an experimental basis. This was a new Army ration. Chocolate did not agree with a number of the troops. The first day, the stash of cookies, crackers and snacks was diminished. Sunday was not a good day. The troops became hungry.

While Bill walked guard duty in a wooded area, he heard a voice saying, "O'Hara, do not turn around." Then, "Just keep walking. We will signal you when we return."

A quick search of the surrounding area revealed nothing. It must have been a joke. Bill continued walking his post. He could hear a radio playing from the cook's tent. The melody was great. For the first time, he heard the musical score from *Oklahoma!* with Gordon McCrae and Shirley Jones singing, "Oh, What A Beautiful Morning".

About an hour later, while still on guard walk, Bill again heard a voice. "Do not turn around but go to the big tree. There is a bag there for you." Again, no one was in sight. Under the tree, Bill found some danish, cookies, an apple and a bottle of Coke. The evidence was devoured and he buried both bag and empty bottle.

Next morning after roll call, all Sunday guard personnel were questioned about any events not reported. Bill stated that he walked his post as required but saw no one come or go from the area. He said that he heard the cook's radio. Apparently, a village official complained to the Commanding Officer that some soldiers bought out the one village store of bread, cold cuts, fruit and other items. He wanted to know why the Army was not feeding its men! Across the formation, questions asked drew only blank looks. One individual, "Al", said he saw some men eating food out of a brown bag on Sunday evening. However, it was his word only and the matter was dropped. Thinking back, the *Oklahoma!* music was as good as the buns and cookies. The chocolate bar experiment was a failure.

In a long letter from home, Catherine informed Bill that Kate was in top shape and all was going well at the house. Kate agreed to be picked up for 7:00AM Sunday Mass at St. John's Church, riding with Catherine and Bill. Up to that time, she had always walked. The boarding house was again filled to capacity.

At the end of October, it was back to Camp Ellis. To the solders' dismay, their former barracks were occupied and they ended up in open fields in tents which held ten, featured grass floors, no lights and no heat. By now, the temperature had dipped and snowflakes were falling. The main goal was to get warm and keep warm. Candles were distributed. For sleeping, it was overcoat and two blankets plus all the clothing one could find. Cots were distributed. Again, red-hot coffee in the mess cup at breakfast was the key to survival. Unfortunately, a large number of troops came down with colds and illnesses. Finally, after about ten days, they got their old barracks back and it was like moving into the Ritz-Carlton.

Ten-day furloughs would soon be available. Bill checked his meager finances and then the train fares to New York. In a telephone call to Kate, he asked for a $20.00 loan, which arrived a few days later. A furlough was granted on November 12, a Friday, at 6:00 PM. However, Bill was required to keep a dental appointment at 7:00 PM. Finally released at 11:00 PM, he and a few of his buddies were driven to Peoria by a soldier friend for $2.00 each. They boarded a Rock Island Railroad train and rode all night to Chicago. No one minded the ride.

Traveling with Bill was Art Wong, a baker. Art had a severe burn scar on one side of his face from a hot baking pan. That, plus his Asian features caused the MP's to check his furlough papers several times over a short period. Back then, feelings were running high against Asians. Finally, Bill and three of the troops told the MP's that Art was one of them and that his papers were in order. The MP's on the train did not again interfere.

It was a thrill to see the NYCRR train waiting in the Chicago station. It was clean and ready to roll. The NYCRR logo on the train looked great. They left at 10:30 AM and although the men stood all the way to Fort Wayne, it was a luxury to travel with other service people and civilians. After finding the dining car, time went swiftly. Soon they passed Buffalo, Rochester and Syracuse. Finally, at 2:00 Sunday morning, the train stopped in Utica. One of the group, Fenton Diefendorf, had to wait until 8:00 for a connection to Fort Plain. Bill asked him home, but he decided to wait at the station.

It was a beautifully clear November morning. Bill walked up Genesee Street and turned onto Hopper Street toward home. Finally reaching the front door, he looked for the key, always hidden out front. No key. He rang the bell, expecting a royal surprise welcome. Soon Kate answered the door, took one look and said, "So that's what you wanted the $20.00 for." With that, she turned and went back to bed.

Bill's room looked exactly as he had left it. He turned in. It was so enjoyable to be home. Suddenly, Bill was being shaken awake. He bounded out of bed in his shorts and dashed into the kitchen. He thought he had missed reveille. Instead, he was staring at an audience of Kate and Catherine, just back from church. The laugh was on him. After a five-star breakfast, he attended the 10:00 Mass at St. John's. It seemed strange to wear a uniform to church. The pastor and a number of friends greeted him.

It was so meaningful to visit everyone. He'd been away only about four months but it seemed like a lot longer. Jack Rowane, Frank Ceiva and Sid Jacobs were all on active duty. The week was filled with dates, movies, dinner out, renewing friendships, visiting family and, best of all, talking with Kate. Bill actually helped with the dishes a few nights, over Kate's mild objections. One evening was spent with Catherine, Bill and little Kathleen. Unfortunately, his leave was to end before Thanksgiving. Kate prepared a turkey dinner in advance with nothing missing. The apple pie was the greatest ever. On another night, Kate invited the family for Irish stew.

Mary's absence, after all these months, could still be felt at home.

On Saturday, a UFA-Proctor football game was the

highlight. Later, a visit to the Stanley Theater found Andy Roy, Manager, still there. All of the ushers Bill knew were in the service. A trip to UFA to see Olive Smith was interesting. Bill told her he was helping to make new history for her classes. Homeroom 120 had not changed. Miss Onderdonk told Bill that she missed his coming in late. She brought him up to date on the location of his former classmates. Bill Price was now a member of the Navy.

The short leave passed quickly and departure time approached. This time, Union Station was quiet. Kate, Catherine and Bill O'Connor were on hand to say goodbye. All knew that this absence would be for a much longer period. And so, at 7:45 PM, Bill, along with several others, boarded the Lakeshore Limited and was off for Chicago. Jack Sears, Ed Mahoney and Don Golden accompanied him. After changing trains at Chicago, they traveled to Macolm, Illinois and finally by bus to Camp Ellis, arriving late Wednesday evening. All were very quiet on the trip back.

Thursday morning formations, drills, hikes and inspections now took place in blowing snow and frigid weather. Rumors of overseas were the order of the day. Bets were on for either England or the Pacific. Each barracks had two potbelly stoves which were kept going full blast. Besides KP and guard duty, the troops also had fireman duty. The fireman fired up the stoves during the overnight hours, keeping wood and coal on hand.

Walking guard duty at three and four in the morning in an Illinois snowstorm left much to be desired. On one such morning, while walking his post in a swirling snowstorm, Bill heard, "Hey soldier, how would you like a cup of coffee?" It was a cook at a nearby Company just going on duty. Bill eased up to the mess hall door and accepted a mug of absolutely the most delicious coffee. He quickly drank it and got back to walking on the street. Sgt. McCorkel appeared out of the dark. Bill went through the routine, "Halt, who goes there? Advance and be recognized." McCorkel wanted to know if Bill had seen the other guard. His answer was negative. He later learned that some guards gathered in a recreational hall in the next area instead of walking their posts. Those involved received severe discipline and extra duty detail. The cook's coffee handout never came up.

That evening, Bill found Corney Klass in his bunk at 6:00 PM, having skipped dinner. Corney could barely talk and was burning up with a temperature. Bill called Sgt. Gossett. The medics came and took Corney to the base hospital. Before he left, he wrote Bill a note. "Call my wife, Marie, in Buffalo. Tell her to come here quickly." Bill found a pay telephone and spoke to Marie. Next evening, Bill visited Corney, now diagnosed with pneumonia. He was happy to learn his wife was en route. The following evening, Bill met Marie and her father who nearly broke Bill's hand with a vigorous handshake. It was a week before Corney was released to limited duties.

Early in October, Bill volunteered to pull duty for his friend, Harry Korman so Harry could observe a Jewish holiday. At Christmas, Harry took over duties so Bill and Ed Mahoney could take a Christmas pass. Ed had just returned from an emergency leave. Both his father and grandfather had died on the same afternoon from heart attacks. On Christmas Eve, Bill called home. The family had gathered at Kate's and all took a moment on the telephone.

A New Year's Eve pass was the last freedom to be

had, although they did not know it at the time. Upon returning to the barracks, they were confined indefinitely.

A new mailing address was issued: APO 709 San Francisco, California. They hadn't the slightest idea where they were headed. Most had figured Europe. Effective immediately, all outgoing mail was to be censored. A considerable amount of preparation went into the next several days. The very last Company formation in front of the barracks would never be forgotten. Over the weeks of training, the guys had always joked about the order, "Fall out with footlockers." This order was actually given, and the troops were laughing so hard, they had difficulty taking the empty foot lockers outside to the trucks.

On a very damp, rainy, January night, the troops boarded trucks to the Camp Ellis railroad area. A few hours later, they arrived in Chicago. Instead of going into the station, they were led through about 1/2 mile of tracks in a drenching downpour. Boarding another train in the dark, the men were directed to take their seats. Away they went. At daybreak, everyone was trying to spot a landmark. For sure, they must have been heading toward the West Coast. After all, they did have a San Francisco APO number. It was difficult to identify a landmark since the shades were kept down. Finally, some of the troops identified a town in Indiana, so they knew they were headed east! Why east when they were scheduled for the Pacific? But then again, the Army did things in strange ways. They were riding on a Pennsylvania Railroad train and finally arrived at Camp Kilmer, New Jersey.

The barracks at Camp Kilmer were clean, warm, two story, and well kept. The food was truly outstanding. It was cafeteria-style with two or three choices of food always available. There were pies, cakes, fruits and no limit to the number of servings. Little did they know at the time but they were in a fattening-up program getting ready for troop ship travel and survival.

Camp Kilmer days consisted of 12 to 15 mile hikes with full packs and equipment. On these hikes, they would see Army Air Corps troops also hiking. They had sloppy packs with clothing and equipment falling on the ground much to their delight but then, they were scheduled to fly, not to be ground soldiers. The New Jersey countryside in winter was beautiful.

One evening, Bill telephoned Kate to advise that he might not be in touch for awhile but not to worry. He would not be able to get home, since twelve hour passes were available and only to the NYC area. He promised to write and keep her informed. Bus service transported troops to 42nd Street and Times Square. Nearby was a gathering spot for servicemen known as the Stage Door Canteen. Coffee and doughnuts were served and entertainment was furnished by Broadway stars and radio personalities. Servicemen from every branch and nation attended. The performer would sit with the troops. The famous lines of the Stage Door Canteen were sung:

"I left my heart at the Stage Door Canteen,
I left it with a girl named Irene."

The words and melody stayed with them for a long time. And the doughnuts were great too.

On Sunday, January 16, Bill traveled to Jack Rowane's home in the Bronx. There, his brothers John, Martin and James visited and Mrs. Rowane, like Kate, put on a fine dinner. Jack's father and sister Anne were also present. Jack was with the Army Air Force in England and his brother Tom was also away in the service.

After a few hours of visiting, it was back to the base. On the following Wednesday morning, January 19, the troops boarded the boat-train and received their last mail delivery for several weeks. A few of them received "Dear John" letters that upset them, since they could not reply. Girlfriend sign-offs were numerous.

Standing dockside next to a large ship, they later learned it was the SS Robin Doncaster, a converted Dutch Merchantman. An Army band played on the dock while doughnuts and coffee were being served by the Red Cross or Salvation Army. The soldiers formed a single line and walked slowly up the gangplank. More than one turned around to take a last look back.

At the tip of the gangplank, a Transportation Officer called each man's last name and the first four numbers of his serial number. The soldier responded with first name, middle initial and his last four numbers. Then it was on to see their living space, six decks below, just over the ship's propeller. "Bunks" were stacked twelve high with little room between. Should a heavy person sleep above, you had a problem. It was now about 5:00 PM, almost dark. No one was allowed topside. The dice and card games started. No one had any idea where the ship was headed.

About an hour later, Bill slipped topside to peek out on the deck. It was a complete black fog, not a light in sight. Visibility was zero. No sooner had he returned but there was a swaying motion. Everyone let out a cheer. They were heading out to sea. K rations were the dinner fare. The men were tired. Bill took the bottom bunk. It was important to keep fingers and elbows in so as not to get stepped on by soldiers climbing up or down the bunks.

Food schedule called for breakfast at 9:00AM and dinner at 4:30 PM. It was a new experience going through all the compartments to the mess area. Very large cooking pots stood about 12 feet high and the stirring utensils looked like shovels and rakes. Breakfast consisted of eggs, toast, coffee and an apple. They were not allowed out on deck. The day was windy and overcast.

The next day brought brilliant sunshine. Jackets and sweaters came off and shirtsleeves were rolled up. It was warmer and the water was a very deep blue as the ship plowed ahead at a good clip. Everyone seemed relaxed. Travel was smooth up to this point. Card games and dice moved to the open decks but no money could be shown. Travel by ship wasn't so bad after all.

The variety of units traveling was a surprise. One of the merchant seamen said the ship boarded some 2,350 troops. The normal complement was around 1,350. Most thought they would be in a convoy. The ship was accompanied only by a small destroyer escort that traveled well out front, barely visible. Sometimes it could be seen bobbing up and down. The following day, the ship sailed near the tip of Cuba and mountains were seen in the distance.

By late afternoon, they neared the Panama Canal. Many remained on deck all night to watch the action. Bill noticed "donkey" motors attached to cables that pulled the ship through the passageways. The "GE" monogram appeared on the side of the motor housing. Areas were brightly lit as a great amount of activity was underway. Workers, trucks, cranes and other equipment were everywhere. The next morning, they'd reached Balboa, the Pacific western-most tip of the canal. Here the ship loaded up on fuel oil and supplies. That night, after dark, it was out into the Pacific to their unknown destination.

The following day was Sunday. The sea had changed and there were deep swells causing the ship to pitch forward, down at the front and up at the back. The sea was grey and the skies overcast. It was announced that a church service would be held in the fantail (rear) of the ship. A chaplain gave a short, inspiring talk. He stood facing the men, his back to the water, which now had a greenish cast. As the ship pitched, the skyline would first appear and then a towering wall of green water. The group was very sober and quiet. They later remembered that service as the talk that took place in front of the green wall.

Sunshine greeted the next day and the troops were treated to new sights. Flying fish leapt out of the water and skimmed the waves. Porpoise swam alongside the ship, diving in and out of the waves. At dark, they saw a glow at the front of the ship from the phosphorescence.

Days began to blend together. Some were sunny, others stormy. Because of the rolling and pitching, many became seasick and were unable to eat. Their friends would bring bread or whatever they could scrounge back to their bunks so they would not go hungry later when they felt a little better. Just the smell of food drove some to the railing. The food itself then became a problem as to quality. The question: were they sick from the sea or sick from the food? Breakfast proved the most reliable.

The officers did not seem to take any interest in the welfare of the Company or its state of health. Rumor had it (and there were always rumors) that no officer in his right mind would appear on deck after dark as it would only take two seconds to help him over the rail.

On the Pacific Ocean, there are two invisible boundary lines. One is the equator and the other the International Date Line. The International Date Line meant that going in a westerly direction, one gained a day. Crossing the equator involved everyone on the ship. All were ordered on deck. Uniform was shoes and shorts. Mops dipped in colored grease painted unsuspecting bystanders. Foot races on the slippery deck, fire hoses loaded with cold salt water gave everyone a bath. There was no place to hide. Boxing matches were arranged on the spot and many a score was settled that day. King Neptune appeared and handed out certificates as proof that all had crossed the equator. Clean up was slow, the troops being limited to cold saltwater showers.

Later that night, the Navy gun crew set up a large screen on deck. All watched a movie and the kitchen sent up cookies, coffee and Kool-Aid. What a day! All that activity kept the men busy and helped make the time pass.

The ship had been at sea, out of the sight of land for over two weeks. One night at about 11:00, ship alarms sounded and the Navy gun crews could be heard firing. The ship must have come under attack. Up the six decks they rushed in no time and stood by their assigned life raft and emergency stations. It was a clear night with a full moon. The firing stopped. It must have been heard for miles. The officers and cadre came by and the troops were dressed down. They were told they were too slow, their water bottles were not kept full, etc. Finally, they were dismissed but few, if any, slept that night. They figured that if there were an enemy sub or ship within miles, it would have heard the firing.

The troops still had not been given a destination. One morning, a ship was seen on the horizon. It was a US Navy oiler and it was very low in the water. It came alongside and fuel lines were connected. As the oiler emptied, it seemed to rise up in the water. Suddenly, Navy personnel began throwing things at the troops. Over the railing came candy bars, cans of fruit, apples and other items. The ship all gave them a cheer. The Navy wasn't so bad after all.

A few days later, they spotted an airplane approaching. Like at Panama, this two-engine plane flew around the ship for over an hour blinking Morse Code. That evening, there were many birds and they knew land, wherever they were, was close by. Over the loudspeaker came the announcement. This was to be New Caledonia, a French colony. The ship entered the harbor area near Noumea but did not go dockside, remaining well away from land. Everyone was expecting to disembark. Their Shipment number was 0841-C. An announcement called for all groups except the 0841-C. A very large, flat barge came alongside and the other troops went down a gangway to the barge. Morale descended a few points.

Suddenly, another announcement: "0841-C, get your 'A' bags only and be on deck in ten minutes!" The men were ready on time and took a seat on the barge that was only clearing about three feet above the water. The harbor was like a millpond. As they started toward shore, the early morning sun beat down. On the side of a hill was a brilliant reflection of a gold color. If at all possible, this would bear investigation.

Bill always wondered what it would be like to land on a foreign shore. He soon found out. Dozens of natives were hawking wares saying, "Hey Joe, one dollah buy necklace or stuffed bird!" The troops boarded trucks to a hillside area and pitched pup tents. This time Bill and

Klass shared a tent in a new climate which was a lot warmer than Illinois. Again, however, no sooner was the tent up than down came the rains. No one minded. It was great to be on solid land. They had to get used to walking without a pitch or roll. The men dug a trench outside and down the middle of the tent. As the water flowed through, they had races with matches or pieces of paper. Foreign lands were so exciting.

The next morning was sunny and permission was given to go into Noumea. Strict orders were to stick together, no isolated straying from the group or going off to the beach. Not all residents were friendly to US troops. Ed Mahoney and Bill toured and checked out all the interesting shops. They slipped away and climbed a very high hill alongside the city. Bill was looking for the source of the bright morning glow. Very near the top of the hill, reachable only by a footpath, was an old abandoned church. On the front of this stone building were two bronze doors, weather-beaten, but giving off a shine in the sunlight. The church inside was in ruins. They quickly made their way back to join the others before being missed. The mystery of the golden glow on the hillside was solved.

After three days, they were back to the ship. While they'd been on land, cargo of aircraft parts, jeeps, trucks and other material was removed. The Doncaster sailed north. Again, their destination was unknown. No one had a guess.

The first night, Bill developed severe stomach cramps and a high temperature that got worse the next day. He could not eat. The drinking water tasted like fish. By the second night, he was unable to stand up alone. Sgt. Gossett and the Company Master Sgt. walked him down to the ship hospital. The medical doctor, a Marine Captain, gave Bill a quick dismissal and began to order a prescription from his medic. The Master Sgt., a 6-foot, 4-inch tower of strength, looked down on the Captain and, in no uncertain terms, told him he expected Bill to be admitted. To fail on this, he would protest loud and clear to the Troop Commander. Bill was admitted.

It was his first time in any type of military hospital. It was the first time he ever saw an intravenous injection. Tom Fey was in the next bunk, quite ill. Both lay there looking up at the bottles swaying back and forth. Neither cared if the ship floated or sank. Others began to arrive. Apparently, the food did not agree with them. By morning, the small clinic was full.

By the third morning, Bill felt better but still could not seem to eat. He was anxious to get back to his group. An announcement was heard. "All troops will prepare to debark this ship in one hour and all will walk off." The medic came by and gave Bill and Tom each a hard fried egg sandwich wrapped in wax paper. It fit into a fatigue pocket for later. The 458th formed up on deck with full field pack, rifle and A and B bags ready to go. About this time, a very offensive odor was detected. It was the result of rotting vegetation from what appeared to be a lush, green paradise island known as Guadalcanal. This was their destination, APO 709. They anchored off shore.

Located in the British Solomon Islands, Guadalcanal was some 45 miles wide and 90 miles long. Twenty miles away was Tulagi. Savo Island could be seen off in the distance. The waterway passage in between was known as the "slot".

Because of treacherous coral, the Doncaster could not

get near shore. There were no docks available. Landing craft bobbed alongside the ship, rising and falling in the swells. The 458th stood on deck with full equipment for a long time, waiting to disembark. Then, it was up to the railing, lift over the A and B bags, drop them onto the landing craft, go over the railing and climb down the rope ladders to the craft below. It was a challenge for those in good shape and a near disaster for others.

In Bill's landing craft, the Lieutenant from the 2nd Platoon was barking orders. One and all disliked him. Bill tossed his bags. They missed the Lt. by inches. All the troops on deck let out a cheer. Everyone made it onto the landing crafts and they churned to the beach of white sand and palm trees. The sun was dazzling. There was not a cloud in the sky and the water was in modest swells. Suddenly, the craft came to a stop, the ramp dropped and "All out!" came the order. The troops stepped off into water up to their armpits (there went the egg sandwich) and, holding rifles up, dragging bags, they walked to shore. Everything began to dry immediately in the hot sun, even the egg sandwich. The troops walked up on the white shoreline with tall palms.

Thirst was a problem. Some troops were dehydrated. The Doncaster drinking water was unfit. The troops found fresh cocoanuts which they opened and drank the cool, sweet milk. This was a big mistake.

By late afternoon, trucks arrived and the 458th was transported up the island. The road was dry and as hard as cement. On both sides were dense growths. Rivers were crossed on wooden trestles that had two sets of planks, each about three feet wide for trucks to navigate. Below were swift flowing waters. The trucks passed Army units living in neat rows of tents. They didn't look too bad. It would not be bad after all, following their long journey on board ship.

At about 6:00 PM, the trucks arrived at a field of incredibly high grass, at least 15 to 18 feet tall. This is called elephant grass. The edges on the blades of this grass were actually razor sharp. The men had arrived at the site of their new home. They vowed not to unpack, for surely, they would not be here very long. In spite of their great basic training, they actually were not in any shape to do much after their experience on the troop ship.

They expected to find their tents. They did. Piled in the grass, they were sopping wet. The fun began. "Let's move it." With this command, the men pulled out the tents and everyone worked to his maximum ability. Unfortunately, the recent intake of cocoanut milk began working overtime as well and it became a challenging affair.

Next, they found a pile of sodden army cots and these were distributed. In the piles of tents and cots, some local bugs, lizards, small snakes and other creatures had set up housekeeping. Adding to the pleasure of their new location were swarms of mosquitoes, delighted to find fresh victims. It then became work, swat, work and swat. As darkness settled in, enough of the six-man tents were erected to house everyone. Cots went up in pitch black; no lights were allowed. A detail dug a temporary latrine, just in time. Food that night consisted of K rations and "bug" juice, a type of Kool-Aid.

Bill and his tent mates dug a ditch around their tent. Many did not. That night, the most fantastic downpour took place. They heard running water. Larry Palladino lit a match and they saw water rushing through the tent taking shoes and light items away. The next morning, everyone searched for shoes, sox and other belongings. Some were never found. They'd kept rifles, gas masks and packs with them in the cots.

The 5:10 AM whistle was back in working order. Many reported in bare feet, some in sox and all were moving slowly. When roll call finished, rifle inspection was announced for next formation. Hot coffee was a good shot in the arm to get started. The troops were served the Army's famous SOS breakfast, their first hot meal in several days. The morning was very damp and actually cool. Rifles were cleaned and then inspected. Everyone fixed up the tents. Some had collapsed in the rainstorm.

Next came a lecture about their surroundings. The island was secure but there could be stray Japanese hiding out in the jungle and hill areas. The men were forbidden to eat anything growing wild like berries, cocoanuts (not to worry), or fruits. Mosquitoes were the real threat to health due to the spread of malaria. Netting and mosquito bars were to be distributed for the cots that night. They were not to drink from the crystal clear streams nearby. Temporary showers of fine cold water were set up consisting of 55-gallon drums on a platform with a faucet at the bottom. This was a luxury after the ship.

An announcement was made that they could write letters. The letters were to be censored. The soldiers could describe their location only as "a southwest Pacific Island". The APO 709 designation guaranteed mail should reach them.

The troops were given a half day off per week. The first Sunday arrived. Ed Mahoney and Bill learned of a Navy hospital chapel three to four miles distance. No transportation was provided for church services. They walked. It had been raining again and the road was a sea of mud. Along came a jeep, splashing down the road. It stopped and a Captain said, "Need a ride?" They got in and headed for the chapel.

The usual question, "Where are you from?" was asked. Ed answered that they'd just arrived and were last stationed outside Peoria, a real soldier's town! He mentioned that Peoria had a great "red light" district and implied that they'd fully enjoyed the city. The Captain let them out near the chapel.

Arriving late, the only empty bench was in the front row. Mass started and when the chaplain turned around to give the sermon, Ed and Bill were shocked. It was the same Captain who had been driving the jeep. He was kind enough not to single them out while he spoke on the Ten Commandments. Following Mass, it was a long walk back, having vowed to refuse all offers of a ride.

The next day, detail was to cut a field out of the dense elephant or kunai grass. Machetes were issued and all day they hacked away. One group began a ditch for drainage. Uniform of the day was fatigue hat, shorts, sox and shoes. The bright sun and high humidity ran streams of sweat. Bill's glasses would simply slide off in the heat. Drinking water consisted of each person's canteen. These were filled in the morning from a "lister" bag hung in the shade. This bag was filled with water from a stream and iodine pills were added. The water was said to be safe to drink after one hour. There being no other source, they drank away. Then, they were loaned out to an Engineering Company to cut more grass, clearing areas for new troop arrivals. Following this duty, they were assigned to transport fuel in 55-gallon drums from the fuel dump. They all needed to be loaded on a 6 by

6-foot truck. Each truck could carry 19 drums. Riding on top of the drums, it was important to keep your fingers free. The drums would crush together in transit. Near the fuel dump was a former ammunition dump that had exploded a few weeks before the 458th's arrival. Trees standing from 80 to 100 feet high had no branches. It was out of bounds, an area of potential danger.

This geographic area had two seasons: the rainy season and the dry season. The rainy season lasted about three months during which time the rains were practically constant, day and night. Brief periods of sunshine would push the humidity to record highs. Roads turned into sludge. Four-wheel drive was the only way for traction. The rain forest never dried out and was never penetrated by sunlight. The decay and rot gave off a most unpleasant odor. Scum covered small lagoons and inland swamps had their share of crocodiles. While sparkling streams looked clean, they flowed through plenty of bacteria upstream.

In April, the 458th moved to a new area alongside a river. The unit put up 14-man tents. Just like the Plaza. The mess tent was located across a stream. A bridge had been built to cross. All were now required to take one Atabrine pill before dinner to protect against malaria. These tended to give one a yellow pallor. Rumor had it that the pill made one sterile. To insure compliance, the Sgt. would watch each troop take the pill and a drink of water. Some were checked with a flashlight. Resentment against this practice was so strong, the inspection stopped. The troops continued taking the Atabrine.

The 458th had several members who could originate information with great confidence and pass it along through the rumor mill. One of these was known as "Whispering Sam". He had the unique ability to effectively communicate data that sounded believable, true beyond question. Sometimes, it was what the troops wanted to believe. "Whispering Sam" was actually Eublio Consalazio but he went by "Eube" for short. He became an authority on rumors - what was fact and what was fiction. At the same time, he had not the faintest idea either way. Ironically, some of his rumors turned out to be true, simply remarkable after all was said and done. It was common to learn of developments from rumors first and from announcements later.

Another unusual individual had been a member of a traveling circus. He was known as "The Tattoo Man". In the shower, he appeared to have been painted from head to toe with animals, snakes, hearts, flags, flowers, names of women and slogans. On the muscle of his right arm was a tattoo of a female. When he flexed his muscle, her hips would wiggle. He was a novelty but somewhat hideous. Most gave him a lot of room.

A truck driver whose last name was Boodrin was known for his ability to get out of detail work. This is known as being a "Gold Brick". His claim to fame was his ability to read comic books. One of his work duties was to burn out the latrines each day. Some were eight, some were twelve holers. After clearing everyone out, he would lift up a seat, pour kerosene in, toss a burning newspaper down and close the cover.

One day, he used aviation gasoline. The newspapers did not ignite but simply smoldered. Soon, a soldier arrived, lifted a cover and sat down to read a paper. As he smoked, he lifted up a cover and tossed his lighted cigarette in. There was a loud "Whoom!" He suffered from severe burns and was taken to the hospital. He had a slight French accent and would describe his injuries in detail. He became a hero of sort with lots of visitors but no Purple Heart was authorized.

One sweltering morning while unloading material from ships, Bill was riding in a DUKW (Duck). This amphibious vehicle had wheels for land and was equipped to put to sea to carrying troops or materials. On one trip back to the beach, the path was blocked by a group of Port Company soldiers. The DUKW came to a stop. There appeared to be confusion. Suddenly, Bill heard a familiar voice barking harsh orders in a vocabulary that left no room for question. Bill leaned over the side of the DUWK and, to his surprise, saw his old UFA track team member, Ted Grimes. Grimes, 5-foot 7-inches, 120 pounds, stood with his hands on his hips ordering his troops about. The group quickly shaped up. They outweighed Grimes two to one but he wore 1st Sgt. stripes.

Bill called down, "Sgt. Grimes, take your choice for the high jump or quarter mile!"

Grimes looked up and immediately flashed his famous smile, overjoyed to see a friendly face. The next Sunday, Grimes visited Bill and they exchanged old times and current developments. Grimes had not seen any other acquaintances from home and was delighted to visit. He was the only high school graduate in his Company. He had worked hard to earn his 1st Sgt. stripes.

One morning, Sgt. Gosset led a group to explore the extreme outer perimeter of the area behind the tents. At one point, they came upon a cocoanut-log gun emplacement. This was a former machine gun nest. The area was heavy with bugs and the troops left shortly. Later, they visited a native village comprised of small thatch huts, incredibly dirty and occupied only by males. The females had all been taken to Savo Island between Guadalcanal and Tulagi.

Disease and illness were evident. The troops were astounded to see men sitting on the ground outside their huts suffering from chronic elephantiasis. They truly were in terrible shape.

During this time, the old UFA group would try and get a few minutes together to compare notes from home. Together, Jack Russell, Joe Giffune, Fran Carney, Don Golden, Jack Sears, Ed Mahoney and Bill had a few laughs. A snapshot was taken and sent to the Observer Dispatch in Utica. Some time later, they received a newspaper featuring their photograph.

One evening, the soldiers walked through the chow line at supper. As usual, it was a downpour. The mess kit was held up for serving and the cook slapped down a big spoonful of food. At the end of the line, another cook spooned out something that resembled Jell-O or pudding. Who could tell? It went "glob", right in the middle of "dinner".

Bill asked, "Couldn't you have at least put that on the side?"

The cook replied, "What's the difference? It's all going to the same place." So much for five star restaurant credits. It was time for one of Kate's home-cooked dinners and pie.

At this point, Sunday church service consisted of Mass being said in a nearby cleared area. The altar was the hood of the Chaplain's jeep. This was near the 217th Signal Battalion area. The priest was a Captain from Baltimore. He always delivered a short, meaningful sermon, talking directly to the troops so far from home. Unfortunately, he became ill and was transported out. The chaplain had been in action up north.

On Guadalcanal was a military cemetery where many hundreds of servicemen had been buried. Each grave was marked with a white cross. Later, all would be moved to the States or to Hawaii. In the center of the cemetery, the natives had constructed a chapel to hold about 100 people. It had a thatch roof, open sides, no doors, and no nails and was held together with logs and vines. It stood as a memorial to those buried there.

The civilian Catholic Bishop from the Solomon Islands and other areas was Thomas Wade. Incidentally, he came from Utica, New York. Bishop Wade had been working in the Southwest Pacific for some 14 years prior to the war. One Tuesday evening, he held a mission service. Permission was given for two 6 by 6 trucks transport. The church was filled to capacity. There were about 250 standing outside. Speakers had been hooked up. The service and the sermon were very meaningful to troops some 9,500 miles from home and looking at a long war ahead.

Bishop Wade spoke of self-sacrifice and told of his early years as a missionary. He spoke about one night while he was paddling up a jungle river in the dark with swarms of mosquitoes and danger of overturning. He said he began to complain of his circumstances. He told that he belonged to the Missionary Order of the Little Flower and in his mind, he began to question its goals and purposes. Finally, when he arrived at his destination, a native village, a great feast had been prepared for him. Elders, children, men and women came to him. Some brought simple gifts and flowers. He said he was both overjoyed and ashamed for having doubted his purpose as a Missionary.

Near the end of his sermon, a torrential downpour started. Not one soldier standing outside moved. This was impressive. The rain came to a stop as quickly as it had started. Bill couldn't believe that no one had left early. He learned that all the drivers were inside, dry, and had no intention of going outside and getting wet.

In early May, Bill and others were unloading a 6 by 6 truck of 55-gallon oil drums. As usual, it was a driving rain and the mud was almost ankle deep. One drum got away over the tailgate and landed across Bill's left foot. Fortunately, he was standing in the mud but damage had been done. Helped under a tree, and with assistance, he hobbled to the nearby mess tent. The Captain ordered his jeep to drive Bill to his tent and ordered sick call for the next morning. It was not a good night and, by morning, the foot was as large as a loaf of bread.

Bill hated sick call since there was always a group of people claiming some type of ailment just to get out of work. He rode in a truck to the 137th station hospital where an X-Ray was taken. There were no broken bones but severe damage to his instep ligaments had resulted. The captain on duty was from Waterville, New York. He ordered no duty for one week. Bill's buddies brought him food and filled his water bottle. Later, they helped him hobble to the mess tent. There were no crutches available.

That week it rained every day and night with no letup. Everything and everyone was soaked. Rivers flooded. Mildew covered shoes and straps and equipment began to rust. All travel on the roads was by four-wheel drive only and at considerable risk. Bill returned to duty but his foot never did seem to go back to its normal size.

It was now the first week of June. The men heard the announcements about the D-Day landings and the invasion. They were excited about this historic event and said a few quiet prayers for the troops involved and for the success of the operation. Although the operation was on the other side of the world, they felt its outcome would have an effect on them. At the time, it was a policy of Europe first and the Pacific second in priority.

TWELVE

DURING HIS TIME off, Bill evaluated his situation and made plans to try and obtain a transfer to some other organization and work. Some units nearby were moving out. One was the 4th Field Artillery Battalion. Bill's friend, Dick Keesler, had just transferred to the 525th QM Group. Dick mentioned an opening for a typist. The last thing Bill desired to be was a typist, but he'd take any port in a storm. Meanwhile, the 4th Field Artillery left. Word came back that they experienced a very high casualty rate.

The following Monday night at 7:00, Bill spoke to Sgt. Gossett, Lt. Glaser and finally to Captain Geiser. His transfer request was accepted and forwarded to Island Command Adjutant Generals' office for approval. They too needed a typist and issued orders transferring him to Headquarters Company, Island Command. Talk about a surprise! Bill knew no one in Island Command, located on the other side of Henderson Field. The organization was headed by Major General Murray with colonels, majors and other brass in abundance.

Bill's buddies all came by to wish him the best. One morning, Captain Geiser and the Company Clerk, Sgt.

Charlie Goff, drove Bill in the jeep to his new location. Actually, they had never been to Island Command and wanted to look it over. All three walked into Headquarters Company's spacious, orderly room. A tall, sharp-looking 1st Sgt. was giving orders from his desk, alternating between a field telephone and a radiogram. The place was at high activity. Standing at his desk, Captain Geiser, Sgt. Goff and Bill were ignored.

Finally, the 1st Sgt. looked up and asked, "What can I do for you?"

Sgt. Goff gave him a copy of the orders of transfer. The 1st Sgt. reached into a pile of papers and pulled out his copy. "Are you O'Hara?" he asked.

Bill spoke up in acknowledgment.

The 1st Sgt. said, "O'Hara, welcome. My clerk will show you to your quarters then report back and I'll explain your work location in the AG office." He turned to the Captain and Sgt. and said, "That's it."

They left. Both looked let down. Neither wished Bill good luck or any word of encouragement on his new assignment.

After stowing his gear in a five-man tent, Bill reported back to the 1st Sgt. He advised him to get lunch and gave directions to the AG Section, reporting to Lt. Leavitt or Capt. Hardy.

Following an early lunch of tasty food, Bill walked to the nearby beach for some quiet reflection. He had left all his friends in the 458th and knew not a single person in Headquarters Company. He meditated and experienced just a little doubt about his decision. He thought about home, of Kate and his life up to July of last year. He hoped that Kate was making it. There was little he could do but was certain that Catherine and Bill would keep an eye on things.

At 1:00 PM, Bill reported to the AG Section, located in a large thatch building, one of several in the complex. 1st Lt. Leavitt was a 6' 4", very friendly officer with a quick smile. His home was in Chicago. Captain Hardy shook hands and welcomed him. Hardy was from Birmingham, Alabama. He was very personable and took Bill around the different groups to get acquainted.

Bill met Frank Christiana from Ilion, New York, not far from Utica. S/Sgt. "Blackie" Bolger came from Chicago, and Fred Siebe from Boise, Idaho. The others all said hello. In the far corner sat Lt. Col. Hilliard, a former professor from Southern California. It was rumored that he spent much of his day composing poetry in Greek for his young wife.

In the building next door was a full "bird" Colonel, Bill Smith, who had a reputation for strict discipline and schedules. A PA system connected the buildings. After some static, Col. Smith's voice would come on with "Col. Hilliard, get over here." Everyone greatly enjoyed these announcements. They confounded Hilliard since he did not know what to expect. Col. Hilliard would jump off his chair and quickly get next door. This always brought plenty of smiles to everyone.

Bill immediately settled down to a volume of typing memos, letters, endorsements, transfers, shipping orders and in no time was well into the maze of paperwork associated with a headquarters operation. At the time, there were about 100,000 servicemen on Guadalcanal. The AG Section initiated the movement orders for individuals and whole organizations in preparation for invasion activities, reorganization, re-grouping and consolidation. Everyone was very helpful. Old typing skills came back quickly. In the days prior to liquid paper correction fluid and electric copy machines, one could go through a case of carbon paper in no time at all. Some reports required up to eight copies. Any more than eight usually required typing the material twice. The manual typewriters took a steady beating from the volume of work. Copy machines required operation of a crank handle to produce copies.

The AG building was constructed of logs, vines and a thatch roof. It had open sides and a wood floor, housing about 20 officers and enlisted men.

Letters from home were always welcomed. In turn, Bill tried to drop notes to family and friends. He wrote Dr. Jim Douglas to express appreciation for all his kindness to the family. About eight weeks later, a package arrived with a return address for Dr. J. Douglas, c/o DeLalla Drug Store, Bleecker Street, Utica. Inside were some 200 packages of Gillette Blue Blades, a very scarce item on the island. There were enough for several tents nearby. A thank you letter was sent to Dr. Douglas, signed by a couple dozen troops.

Bill's tent mates were Blackie Bolger, Bob Sweeney from Bucyrus, Ohio, Curley Merritt from Battle Creek, Michigan and Mel Pagel of Detroit. Mel was 1st Sgt. of the AG Section. At night, a card game always got underway. One small candle was allowed.

Located about 1-1/2 miles from Henderson Field, they could hear the night fighters warming up and roaring down the runway. Sometimes, they heard the engines sputtering and coughing. Bolger had the best ears. When he would drop his cards and race to the ditch, the others followed and he was usually right. One night, there was a submarine alert and the men didn't go too far from the ditch all night.

Each week, everyone received a half-day off though sometimes, a peak workload such as a major shipment of troops required around-the-clock effort.

One morning, Bill was trying to hitch a ride to the Red Cross Center. It was important to step back if a Marine or Navy vehicle came along. Being Army, one could be run over. Soon, a jeep pulled up and a voice said, "Get in." It was Col. Bill Smith! He said, "I've seen you around the AG office, where's your home?"

Incredible as it sounds, Bill and the Colonel had a great, informal chat. The Colonel asked about Bill's schooling and about his plans after the service. He asked Bill's opinion regarding the Red Cross Center.

Next thing they knew, the jeep came to a halt and Col. Smith began talking with the Commanding Officer of the Guadalcanal and Tulagi Naval Operation. He was heading the opposite way on the same road. Bill saluted and walked the remaining distance. From that day on, whenever Bill brought material to Col. Smith's office, it was not uncommon for him to be called by name.

Dick Geddes, a former member of the 458th, transferred to the Inspector General (IG) section near Bill and became a court reporter. Dick came from St. Paul, Minnesota. He was qualified in both shorthand and typing. His work became a real challenge. In a great number of courts martial cases, he would be up half the night transcribing his dictation, all taken by hand. The system required eight copies. The IG did not like typing errors. A mistake meant correcting nine sheets. Dick was promoted to T-3 (S/Sgt.). He had earned it.

For recreation, there was the ocean for swimming and the beach for ball games, horseshoes and hiking. Nearby was a swift flowing wide stream with crystal clear fresh water. To their dismay, the men found that, after a few swims in the stream, they broke out with skin and nail problems. Dick was diagnosed with a case of fungus of the eardrum. This gave him terrible discomfort. The streams and rivers were declared off limits. However, the infections were to remain with the troops for many years. All they could do was try to keep it under control.

One Saturday night, Bill and his tent mates went to the boxing matches. It was usually a match between a Marine and a soldier or sailor. Once, Bill identified a Marine boxer as Joe Miller, Bob's brother, and a neighbor from home. He contacted Joe who came to the Headquarters Company on a Sunday. Joe was in the 1st Marine Division and had seen much action.

They took lunch in the mess hall. Eyes went up when a Marine walked in. Joe thought the meal was delicious. His Company had lots of activity and their food wasn't the best. Joe was a machine gun squad sergeant. A couple years ahead of Bill, Joe had played as quarterback on the UFA football team. Bill introduced Joe to his tent neighbors. They had a great visit.

Later, Bill always thought it best that one could not predict the future. Joe fought in new Marine invasions. After the war, he joined the sales force of the Bossert Company. He married and started a family. When the war broke out in Korea, he was called up in the Marine reserves. His unit was last seen in action around the Chosin Reservoir in North Korea. He never returned.

Bill helped Larry Palladino transfer to Headquarters

136

from the 458th. Soon after Larry arrived, he received a package from his mother back in Manhattan. Wrapping paper and string were loose. The guys saw a big loaf of homemade Italian bread sticking out from the package. It had started to mold. Everyone suggested Larry toss it. Instead, he hung it on a tent strap and greased the strap to keep bugs away.

Soon it was Christmas Eve. Larry split open the bread. Inside was a long, narrow bottle of white liquid. It was homemade anisette, probably 190 proof. He poured a small amount for Dick and Bill and suggested, "Just sip, don't drink it." He was right. The three friends sat up half the night sipping, taking a break for Midnight Mass. They walked the beach looking at the fantastic star patterns of the Southern Hemisphere. They saw the Southern Cross but no Big Dipper or other stars of the Northern Hemisphere. They felt so far removed from the snow and cold.

Blackie Bolger and Fred Siebe made a Christmas tree out of a tent pole by drilling holes and sticking coconut palm branches in them, all painted silver. There were no lights or decorations but the tree drew a lot of laughs. Bolger threw a little party. He had saved up his 3.2 beer and offered peanuts along with a stack of sardine sandwiches with onion slices. In the weeks that followed, Bolger made friends with the cook. The cook would call the guys to his corner where he'd have a brown bag of oven baked rolls, some meat (although no one knew what kind) and cake. It was a real treat. On Christmas Day, the cook put out a fine meal with everything he had at his disposal. He even baked rolls and made up flat tray apple pies. This helped lift their spirits on December 25.

About three evenings a week, the soldiers traveled

up the island to the 27th Seabees or to the Navy unit for a movie. Westerns were popular. War movies did not go over too well. On Sunday afternoons, touch football on the wide beach or a softball game used up time. The island was about 90 miles long and 45 miles wide but with no travel inland. There were active volcanoes and swamps in the jungle, soft ground, muck, and some quicksand, all of which catered to a variety of reptiles, bugs, snakes and other unidentified inhabitants. Also, there was an abundance of wild pigs. These were very dangerous. Troops would stick to no more than one-half mile inland from the shore. There were gold mines inland but no one thought they were worth the risk to search. On the coast, travel was limited from Point Cruz and Lunga Point and to Koli Point up-island.

On one bright, sunny morning, en route to Tulagi on a PT boat, Bill thought he'd ride up front with his back to the windscreen. Going out of the harbor was great. Nice breeze. Once out in the "slot", it got quite choppy and the PT boat rose and fell in the swells. There was nothing to hang on to except the edge of the windscreen. About one foot above the front edge of the PT was an emergency rope. It ran around the front edge of the boat. After 20 miles of rising and falling, they reached Tulagi Harbor.

A sailor asked if Bill had enjoyed the ride. "Absolutely," he replied.

It took an hour to stop shaking. En route back to Guadalcanal later that day, Bill rode inside. Tulagi was 99 percent Navy but otherwise resembled Guadalcanal.

Around October, the Headquarters moved to another location with newly erected small wood-frame buildings. No more dirt floors! Until now, it had been a steady diet of tents. This was a great improvement. Each building held about 40 soldiers. At this time, Bill was promoted to T-5 (equivalent to Corporal) and was followed soon thereafter to T-4 (Sergeant).

Meanwhile, the AG Section was extremely busy with troop movement orders for actions planned up north. Located nearby, the 137th Station Hospital was filled with wounded brought back by hospital ships from action up north. There were no ambulance air transport or helicopter evacuation units in those days.

Greatly increased air activity was evident. Fighters and bombers were flying at all hours. When returning, sometimes flying very low, ground troops could see large holes in the airframe fuselage. Some engines would be smoking. At times, wheels could not be lowered and the plane in trouble would head for nearby "Lunda Lagoon" and ditch. The Navy would immediately hook on to the stricken aircraft before it sank. Following crew rescue, necessary salvage for the spare parts got underway. After dark, flights of P-38 aircraft would zoom overhead at treetop level, heading off to spoil someone's evening.

The 124th Army Ground Forces Band was assigned to the headquarters of General Murray. Bill met several members, one of whom was Joe Zebrowski from Stamford, Connecticut. Every Monday at 7:00 PM, a full dress formation was held. With the band playing a march, the Company would head for the main flagpole and retreat ceremony. The 124th always did an outstanding job with a top performance.

Each morning around 10:00, Bill took about ten minutes for a trip to find some coffee and to scan the bulletin board. Everyone worked with sleeves rolled up. While reading the board, a voice said, "Soldier, what is your name and to whom do you report?" Bill turned and snapped to attention for Major General Murray, recognizing him by the stars on his collar.

Bill saluted and answered his questions. The general told him to roll down his sleeves and gave a short lecture on proper wearing of the uniform. He then loosened up a bit, asked for hometown, how long he had been serving and a few other items of light conversation. Out of the corner of his eye, Bill noticed some of his associates, both enlisted and officers, giving the bulletin board area a lot of distance.

Finally, General Murray said, "You are excused." Bill saluted and left. The guys couldn't wait to learn what that was all about including Major Schiff, the AG Section Officer. It was noted that all personnel lowered sleeves after leaving work areas.

Assigned to the AG Section was Warrant Officer Junior Grade (WOJG) Richard Burnham. A former Master Sergeant, Burnham taught Bill how to cut through Army paperwork, truly a world in itself. He taught policy, procedures, chain of command, instructions and correspondence.

Burnham had been overseas for three years and was granted a 45-day furlough to New Zealand. He took requests from many on items they wished him to purchase. He flew out of Henderson Field in a twin engine C-47 loaded with cargo and mailbags. He said later that the plane never got higher than a few thousand feet and it strained all the way to make it. Burnham spent his time in Wellington and from his appearance upon return, must have had a great furlough. He brought back all that was ordered.

He came from a small town in Pennsylvania. In the

work group, Captain (later Major) Hardy, 1st Lt. Leavitt and WOJG Burnham comprised an outstanding team with which to serve.

Recreational activities included evening softball, day or late afternoon ocean swimming or fishing. No swimming was allowed after 6:00 PM since the sharks usually put in an appearance. They weighed around seventy-five pounds and had blue noses. One of the cooks would row out in an old dinghy and toss some old meat attached to a cable and hook into the water. He carried a butcher block and hatchet. If whatever he caught became overwhelming for him, he simply chopped the cable.

One evening, the soldiers heard him calling for help. He was rowing for shore. Several went to the shore and helped pull the dinghy on land. The cable was positioned over a tree branch. A large stingray was pulled out of the water. It was shaped like a big, upside-down saucer, several feet across, black, with one eye and a long whipping tail. Halfway down the tail was its venomous spine, which appeared razor-sharp. After a brief look and a few snapshots, the stingray was let back down into the water. The sharks took over from there.

At the bulletin board again one morning, Bill was astounded to see a three by five card with a black border which read," President Roosevelt died at Warm Springs, Georgia, April 12. He is succeeded by Vice President Harry S. Truman." That name was new to the troops but they soon learned all about him.

Two days later at 1:00 PM, all work came to a stop. The entire Company met in formation. The formal announcement of the death of the President was made. Every officer and enlisted man in Headquarters Company AG

Section was present. The AGF Band played a slow-step funeral march and everyone proceeded to a cleared field near the headquarters flagpole. To the strains of the martial music, several cannons were fired. The flag was lowered and raised with appropriate ceremony. The details and meaning of the ceremony were never explained but it took place on the same day of the President's funeral.

The ceremonies took about an hour and a half from start to finish. The hot sun caused a few of the troops to topple over. Later, they learned that every serviceman in every branch on the island participated in memorial ceremonies that afternoon. As the ceremonies ended, the band again played a solemn march back to the living area. The troops then reported back to their duties. Their new Commander in Chief was Harry S. Truman.

The troops on Guadalcanal followed the war in Europe with keen interest especially during the first four months of 1945.

Finally, the announcement arrived that General Eisenhower had accepted the German unconditional surrender at Rheims on May 7, 1945. Europe had been first, the Pacific was next. This now put all priorities on the defeat of Japan.

Although great news, there was little celebrating. At the time, it still looked like a long drawn-out affair to finally beat Japan.

News events were reported for the troops by the Armed Forces Radio Network which provided excellent coverage as well as a variety of good music. Bing Crosby, Jo Stafford, Glen Miller, Freddie Martin and others were regulars. The STARS AND STRIPES weekly newspaper and YANK magazine helped fill the gap from regular newspapers. Characters like "Sad Sack" and "Willie and Joe" helped brighten the day. Newspapers from home were about six weeks old but got passed around for all to read. "I'll Be Seeing You," was a popular song.

USO shows would bring Jack Benny, Jack Carson and Bob Hope with Jerry Colonna and a few charming ladies. These were always entertaining and gave morale a lift. MP units were on hand to maintain order at the shows.

In the early fall, Headquarters Company consolidated and again moved. This time, it was back up the island near Henderson Field where the 9th Station Hospital had vacated to move north. General Murray, Major Hardie, Lt. Leavitt and WOJG Burnham, along with the 124th AGF Band, all moved off the island, assigned to new duties. Geddes, Palladino and Bill now shared space in a thatch building about 500 yards from the shore. The ranking AG Section Officer was Lt. Col. Charles G. Geduldig from Seattle. He was an excellent leader and knew his business one hundred percent.

Bill was next promoted to T-3, equivalent to Staff Sergeant. A few times a week, Colonel Geduldig sent him to meet the NATS (Naval Air Transport Service) plane to deliver classified documents or to pick up documents. If the material was classified top secret, an armed MP rode with Bill. On many visits to NATS flights, the crew would hand Bill a few newspapers only three days old from the states. On sunny days, the trip was a pleasure driving the jeep. In a downpour, it was four wheel drive and full concentration to stay on the road. One of the highlights of the trips to Henderson was the Sgt. accepting shipments. He was from Liberty Bell, Texas. He kept a framed picture of his girlfriend nearby. She was a knockout. He hoped she waited for his return.

One of Bill's responsibilities was the preparation of travel orders. On one occasion, Bishop Thomas Wade came by for orders. On yet another time, travel orders were cut for a member of the Coast Watcher organization. This elite group of men lived on the islands behind Japanese lines and acted as the eyes and ears that were needed to radio messages on aircraft and ship movements to give the US forces time to get ready. Most coast watchers were Australian or New Zealanders. Some had formerly run plantations on the islands. They were instrumental in saving the lives of many downed airmen and shipwrecked sailors. The war had now moved far to the north so they were all coming out.

Just prior to the move to the 9th Station area, an incident took place in which many casualties resulted. The troops were awakened during early hours one morning by a tremendous blast. It felt like having your ears slapped. This was a concussion from a ship up the island that had been loading torpedoes. The ship exploded and pieces of hot metal from the deck and elsewhere began to fall. The troops headed for the ditch one more time. The members of an entire Port Company were lost. Saved were two sailors who were on the ship's fantail. A 6:00 AM reveille was called and the men loaded on to trucks for the explosion area. The Company was assigned to look for bodies on the shoreline and in the water. It was a long and depressing day. The Chaplain and Graves Registration Unit had their work cut out for them. The cause of the disaster was never learned but it was not credited to enemy action. "Tokyo Rose" was on the air that week claiming credit. The loss of the ship was considered accidental.

A visit with Bill Strawson and Corney Klass back at the 458th QMC found them packing for a move north, destination as usual, unknown. They were gone in a couple of weeks, and landed at Saipan and the Tinian Islands, now secured. Ed Mahoney wrote telling of sand, heat, sun, no trees and the same food.

Bill had been corresponding with a few of his high school friends. One was Fred Owens. At home, their backyards met. Fred had poor eyesight but persisted in getting into the service. His father was Dr. Frederick T. Owens. On more than one Halloween, Fred and Bill would have plenty of tricks for the neighbors, all in good taste. Fred entered the Army in August 1943, assigned to the Infantry.

In a mail call sometime in November 1944, Bill found a letter returned to him that he had mailed to Fred. A small circle was stamped on the envelope. Inside the circle were the letters "KIA". The mail orderly told Bill that his friend was killed in action and he expressed his regrets. Soon thereafter in a letter from Catherine, Bill received a copy of the news article on Fred.

He was killed in action November 19, 1944 on Leyte. He had trained at Camp Wheeler in Macon, Georgia and at Fort Ord, California. He last was home on furlough in November 1943 before sailing to New Guinea. Others in the Company expressed regrets to Bill when they learned he had lost a friend. Fred was buried at Arlington Cemetery.

Kate was upset over the loss of Fred Owens, living so close to home. Otherwise, according to Catherine, Kate was plugging along serving great meals, baking and adjusting around meat and food shortages. Later, Bill found some invoices made out to Kate by the G. Petrotta Company, 421 Bleecker Street:

10 1/2 Lbs. Pork Chops @ $ .30 Lb.	$3.05	6-7-44 Inv.
9 3/4 Lbs. Corn Beef @ $. 30 Lb.	$2.93	
10 Lbs. Boneless chuck @ $ .35 Lb.	$3.50	6-10-44 Inv.
7 1/2 Lbs. Spare Ribs @ $ .25 Lb.	$1.88	

It would appear that all were being served hearty meals. The meat and potatoes plus vegetables, biscuits and apple pie kept them coming back for more. Catherine and Bill O'Connor stayed in close contact with Kate.

One of the more tragic happenings on the island was the number of soldiers' deaths by their own hand, usually by hanging. For unknown reasons, these usually took place on Sunday afternoons. Depression, discouragement, unfavorable news from home, or just plain helplessness may have been reasons.

Earlier in the fall, all females including nurses and Red Cross workers were shipped off the island. Only two Australian Red Cross females remained and they later left.

Bill came into contact with Australian and New Zealand servicemen. The New Zealanders were all tall and in addition to height, wore a campaign hat that folded over on one side, giving them an even taller appearance. They would trade anything for some 3.2 American beer.

One evening, some New Zealand sailors rowed a small boat ashore to visit the PX. They were all very friendly and wore flat, round hats. It was difficult to understand them although they were supposed to be speaking English. The aircraft from their small carrier flew in for service and refueling. All of these servicemen appeared very capable of standing up well in action.

Every headquarters generated a volume of paperwork. It was important to be able to locate from the file on short notice. The Army had its system for filing which followed the Dewey System. One S/Sgt. in charge of records used the Army system. In addition, he initiated his own. For every originating correspondence, the S/Sgt. would take one carbon copy and place it face-up in a stack. There were some five or six stacks about as high as a filing cabinet with a heavy weight on top of each. Whenever the Army system failed to locate a key document, the S/Sgt. went into one of his stacks and never failed to eventually locate the paperwork. His key ingredient was a date. He guarded his thatch building like Fort Knox. Canvas tent drops were placed on the sides to keep out the rain.

Bill was next promoted to Technical Sergeant (three stripes on top and two on the bottom). He now had a total of 48 reporting to him and put to full use all of the orientation and training furnished him by WOJG Burnham. Troop movements accelerated with greater numbers moving to the north. Offshore would be dozens of merchant and Navy ships forming convoys to head north.

The men never did adjust to the changes in the weather cycles. In spite of the high humidity and tropical heat, early mornings could be very damp and slightly on the cool side. Dampness created mold everywhere. Shoes not worn for a few days began to turn green. Frames for eyeglasses, even the metal part covered by plastic, turned green. Everyone tried to get into some sunshine daily just to get the feel of heat on his bones. This, however, planted sunspots on the skin that showed up later in life. The sun could completely dry out a soaking shirt in about an hour.

The sun helped dry out the roads. The Seabees loved the sun. Henderson Field first received crushed coral as a runway base. But the coral kept sinking in the muck. Interlocking steel mesh was laid down and some layers also sank out of sight. Most aircraft were single-seat fighters with twin-engine bombers as well. On one occasion, a large four-engine bomber landed but immediately refueled and took off. There was concern that it would be too much weight for the runway.

One morning, the Headquarters Company clerk informed Bill that Lt. Michael Borod and 1st Sgt. William Itkin wanted to see him. A summons like this usually meant bad news. Upon arrival, Bill was put at ease. He was given a sales pitch by Lt. Borod to consider filling out an application for Warrant Officer Junior Grade (WOJG), the same rank as Dick Burnham. The position would be filled on premises and assignment would be in the AG Section. A 45-day furlough would be granted. However, an additional two-year period of service would be required. Bill declined. If he had accepted, the trip home would be immediate.

Next, Sgt. Itkin talked to Bill about the possibility of Transportation Corps Officer Candidate Training School (OCS). The 90-day training period would be stateside and again, a 45 day furlough would be granted. Again, Bill declined interest. He made it very clear to both that if this opportunity had presented itself earlier, he certainly would have been interested. He expressed his sincere appreciation for their having considered him.

It was now mid-1945 and replacements began arriving from the states. Bill began to orient and train as WOJG Burnham had done for him some months ago. Lt. Col. Geduldig transferred out and was replaced by a regular Army major who had been stationed in Australia throughout the war. He was the new AG Officer. He was totally

148

unqualified for his assignment. He simply did not know the policies and procedures and would not listen to recommendations. The operation started to falter. It took a concerted effort and long hours to keep things straight.

Guadalcanal had become a rear-echelon supply base. The Japanese remained at Bouganville, a few hundred miles to the north, where they would hold out until the end of the war.

In early August, the soldiers learned about the atomic bomb being dropped. They knew the end should be soon. World newspaper headlines on August 7, 1945 announced that an atomic bomb had been dropped on Hiroshima and on August 9, that an atom bomb hit Nagasaki.

Finally, on August 16, newspapers across the world carried bold print headlines of the Japanese surrender, ending the war.

The AG office housed a Teletype machine. Whenever an important message or a priority communication was sent, a bell would ring to get attention and action. As the declaration of surrender was transmitted, the bell started to ring and did not stop for about an hour, long after the message had been received. Everyone gathered. All work came to a halt.

The troops were given the remainder of the day off. Stores of hidden 3.2 beer appeared. The mess hall opened up and served the best food available. After so long, it was hard to believe that it was actually over. Bill got off an airmail letter to Kate and to Catherine informing them that his months would be numbered.

Many of Bill's former associates had left including Bolger, Siebe and others. In September, the Army announced a point system for discharge. Soldiers received two points for each month of active service. In addition, combat points were awarded. Bill had about 50 points and no combat awards so it would be a case of wait and see. Men 38 years and older were given priority.

Dick Geddes qualified to ship out in November. Frank Christiana and Bill went to the ship to see him board. Dick would eventually get back to St. Paul, Minnesota. A few weeks later, it was Frank's turn to board a ship. Larry Palladino and Bill saw him off.

That Christmas was the third one away but it was a happy one with the war over and expectations of leaving (finally) for home. Larry and Bill went to Midnight Mass. At about midnight, a few Navy ships in the harbor let go with gunfire to help celebrate the holiday. Again, the men sat up and talked half the night. It would have been worth $100 to be able to make a couple of telephone calls.

The first week of January found the AG Section making a final move to an area near Henderson Field. The new Major continued in charge and it was simply a case of getting by one day at a time. Bill continued deliveries to NATS. He noted that the roads and bridges were deteriorating. After he returned one day, Larry was waiting for him with a big smile.

"I've got great news. How would you like to type your travel orders for stateside?" he asked.

Orders would be issued for a number of troops to be shipped out at the end of the month. The men were walking on air. Sure enough, the next day, the orders were compiled and Larry and Bill each typed their own names on the document. The Movement Order read in part:

"The following Enlisted men will proceed to the
U.S. starting 28 Jan 46 by FAGWT* and be pro-

cessed for release from service in accordance with regulations." *(First Available Government Water Transportation)

The days were a drag up to January 28. Bill sent an air mail letter home to stop writing and that he would telephone as soon as he could after arriving stateside.

On the 28th, Bill, Larry and others were transported to the ship, a Navy APA carrier making a trip south from islands up north. They boarded with their one green bag that held all of their worldly possessions. The A and B bag system was no more. What a difference they experienced from the feelings two years prior to arrival at Guadalcanal. The ship was able to dock, therefore, making it easy to board. Below decks, the troops once again took a bunk, one of twelve stacked to the ceiling. Back up on deck, they watched the ship's activity of getting underway.

Standing in parade formation near the dock was a contingent of troops from the Gilbert Islands. They wore tan uniforms, short sleeve shirts, short pants, had bare feet and looked very sharp. At a signal from the officer in charge, they began a series of songs, mostly like a chant. They continued through the ship's departure whistle. The APA carrier very slowly backed away from the dock and continued slowly away from shore. It followed a very narrow channel between the coral. Still able to see the Gilbert Islanders, the troops couldn't hear them. Finally, the ship came about and started forward, heading north around Cape Esperance and around the western side of the island, then south. It was announced that their destination would be New Caledonia. No troops were to be allowed off ship but no one cared since they were headed home.

The trip to New Caledonia took about 2 1/2 days and was a far cry from the same journey of 1944. The APA carrier had a military order about it but a relaxed atmosphere. Bill was assigned responsibility for some personnel to walk guard and fire-watch detail. Two meals a day were served and the food was actually good. Compared to the SS Robin Doncaster, it could be rated as excellent. The ship had been involved in transporting personnel for island invasion campaigns in the north.

At Noumea, New Caledonia, the ship was tied up dockside. Cranes and equipment moved a great amount of equipment. Additional troops boarded. The regular Navy crew was granted their first liberty in a number of weeks. They left dressed in whites. Larry and Bill remained on deck most of the night. It was somewhat startling to actually see females on and around the docks, the first they'd seen in about a year and a half.

Liberty for the Navy personnel was up at midnight. Around 11:30 PM, sirens could be heard coming from the city. Flashing red lights, police whistles and a din of noise appeared just behind a number of sailors who dashed up the gangplank, paused to salute and then disappeared below. They were then followed by more, all in a considerable hurry to get aboard. Next, jeeps arrived with Shore Patrol and MP's accompanied by sailors who were having some difficulty walking a straight line.

Local police arrived on the scene. They were looking for some sailors who had caused damage and trouble in the city. Lively discussions took place at the foot of the gangplank. In the middle of this, a truck arrived loaded with returning sailors wearing formerly white uniforms. Finally, all got back on board and things quieted down.

The ship then took on fuel and at daybreak, set sail for San Francisco.

The troops were in very high spirits. The second day out, while standing alongside the railing, Bill saw a familiar face and called out, "Bunk Noonan, is that you?"

A sailor turned and came back to shake hands. Jerome "Bunk" Noonan and Bill had been friends in school. Noonan had played basketball for St. Francis de Sales. He was on duty but promised to talk with Bill again soon.

Later that day, Noonan took Bill to the Navy break area and served him his first bottle of Coca-Cola since 1943. There was a very small gym and Noonan insisted that Bill try shooting a few hoops. One shot looked perfect but Bill missed by two feet. No sooner had he thrown the ball than the ship's motion caused the hoop to move away. They had a good laugh. Bunk told Bill to call on him if he could be of any help on their journey.

A new acquaintance was John Mahoney from Lynn, Massachusetts, near Boston. He had been on the island for some time and, along with everyone else, was looking forward to getting back.

The ship moved along at a fast pace but experienced some very rough weather. About five days out, the seas became totally unreasonable for the landlubbers. As before, all interest in food vanished. John Mahoney was an expert on the prevention of seasickness. He recommended they stand as close to the funnel on the ship as possible. Here, he said, was the least roll movement. It did not seem to help very much.

Normally, the mess hall served the troops in shifts. They received a metal tray and coffee mug and sat at long tables. As the weather worsened, they took their food in a bowl, hung onto it and tried to eat by spoon. To let it go, the bowl would slide down the table to the deck. As one end of the table went up, the opposite side was well down. Bets were made to determine just how far the ship could safely roll. More than once, the men would look up at the top of the mast to see how far it would swing from left to right in the rolls. Finally, the weather let up. Even the sailors were glad.

Some of the days in the bright sunshine and deep blue ocean were breathtaking for those who lived on land. At night, the stars were incredibly bright. Soon the Southern Cross was gone and they once more saw the Big Dipper. Again, they watched schools of flying fish. There were many porpoise. Sometimes shark fins could be seen behind the ship.

About a week from California, they noticed a change in temperature. Out came their field jackets that had not been worn in a couple of years. A few days from the coast, the troops heard over the PA system their first stateside music played by the Freddie Martin Orchestra and it sounded absolutely great.

An announcement stated they would arrive at San Francisco the next morning. No one slept that night. The rail was lined at daybreak. At dawn they could barely see the outline of land. It slowly took shape. Far off in the distance was the Golden Gate Bridge. Having sailed to Guadalcanal by way of Panama in 1944, the men hadn't seen this before. It seemed strange but, as the ship approached to go under the bridge, it appeared that there wouldn't be much clearance. How wrong they were. The bridge looked a mile high as the APA carrier passed underneath.

The ship tied up dockside. The men saw the hills of the city close to the harbor. Orders were given to disembark and they were ready. It was exhilarating to walk down the gangplank and step onto U.S. soil. Formation was called to order. They marched about a half-mile along the dock with their green bags slung over one shoulder. As totally unbelievable as is may seem, they boarded another ship. This time it was a large riverboat for a two hour ride up the Sacramento River to Camp Stoneman. It was actually pleasant, a smooth ride after their long voyage. Everyone was in a chipper mood.

Right behind their boat was another loaded with troops. The men were dressed in winter olive-drab uniforms. They covered every inch of space, sitting on the deckhouse roof and other exteriors. Not one of them waved or moved. They were a solemn-looking group. Later, it was learned that they had just returned from duty in Korea.

Camp Stoneman couldn't have been better. The soldiers were assigned barracks which were all neat and clean. The place reminded them of Camp Ellis. Immediately, everyone hit the HOT FRESH WATER showers. Next was a trip to the mess hall. Like Camp Kilmer, there were two or three choices available for dinner. The first fresh milk in two years was served. Real potatoes, fresh baked bread (minus the insects), and other items made it a super welcome-home meal.

The telephone exchange was their next stop. This proved to be an unexpected challenge. A very attractive young lady operator greeted Bill with a smile and requested his calling number. He was not able to respond. It was the first young lady he had tried to speak to in many months.   Instead, he wrote out the number to Utica: 4-1728.

Kate was not at home.   Tim Smiddy heard the telephone ring and headed downstairs to answer it.   Bill told him he would try and call the next night or in about a week from Fort Dix, New Jersey, his next and final destination.

The following day involved a partial physical and initial paperwork for separation.   In a group meeting, the men were informed that any service-related injury could be claimed but that it would result in a longer out-processing schedule.   No one declared anything.   A presentation was made on the advantages of re-enlistment or to sign up for active Army Reserves.   Present rank would be maintained, a monthly paycheck would be offered and assignment would be made to a local unit of the National Guard where one lived.   No one signed.

The men were notified that their group would board a train leaving that night at 7:00 for Fort Dix.   Imagine having been informed of a destination!   No one was late for the train.   Larry and Bill were up front to board.   This turned out to be a mistake.   They were assigned to the first car on the train, immediately behind the steam locomotive and coal tender.   They didn't mind a bit although several days later, upon arrival, all troops in that car wore a mantle of coal dust.   Their coach seats were straight up and not made of straw.   There were no complaints.   The train traveled through New Mexico, Arizona, a bit of Texas, up through Kansas and into Chicago.   Next, they hooked on to a PRR locomotive for the trip east.

It was a troop train setting but a relaxed atmosphere. The Transportation Corps was in charge.   Mess kits were used for meals which were quite good with fresh foods, milk and fruits. The first major stop was at the station in Albuquerque, New Mexico. Permission was granted to leave the train for fifteen minutes but the station was off-limits. It was a beautiful, cool and refreshing day. It was also the very first time in two years that the troops had set foot into civilization.

Everything looked like heaven. On the platform was an oversized four-wheeled wagon loaded with candy bars, fresh fruit, cold drinks, newspapers and magazines. Once spotted, the troops descended on the poor man selling these goods like the Guadalcanal mosquitoes had zeroed in on them. In no time, he was practically sold out. With no time to make change, the troops simply tossed money at him, more than enough. The train whistle blew and off they dashed aboard the train. A few ended up trotting alongside until the last minute. They had current newspapers, cookies, candy and fruit. Who could ask for more?

To fight boredom, Bill walked to the back of the train, now traveling through Kansas. He went out on the very back platform. The door opened and the conductor came out, took out his pocket watch and observed the telegraph poles going past. He explained that he was checking on the speed of the train to see if they would be on schedule. He clocked the train at 78 miles per hour. Bill told him his name and that he had worked for the NYCRR Signal and Freight Departments while in school. The conductor was very interested and said that he had over 40 years with the railroad.

While still in Kansas, the train came to a stop in the middle of nowhere at about midnight. The engine needed to take on water and load up on coal. The stop was a half-hour long. Bill and Larry were awake and stepped off the train to stretch. Other troops also got off the train. They were pleasantly surprised to find a Salvation Army unit standing in the cold February night serving coffee and doughnuts. The Salvation Army workers would not accept any money. However, one of the troops passed the hat and a generous contribution was made. Their act of kindness was remembered in the years to come through the numerous contributions that these same troops made to this fine organization. Someone was heard to say, "What made this so good tonight was the fact that we had our first U.S. doughnut," a truly unexpected treat.

After Chicago, the trip seemed to speed up. At one location known as the Great Horseshoe Bend, it was possible to look back and see a portion of the train still going around the bend.

Finally, they arrived at Fort Dix. After assignment to a temporary barracks, they were issued a set of winter clothing including a heavy jacket. Out-processing got underway. The paymaster settled with each soldier on an individual basis for pay, his rank, travel allowance to his home location and any outstanding claims.

The coveted Honorable Discharge came next along with papers on insurance matters and a form letter of appreciation from President Harry S. Truman.

The date was March 1, 1946 when they stepped out of the Army. As Larry and Bill departed, they ran into a group from the old 458th QMC. All left Fort Dix together, found a small tailor shop and got pressed up a bit. Stripes and insignia were sewn on correctly and next it was a train to New York City. Upon arriving at Penn Station, they headed to a restaurant for a goodbye drink. There were five present and all insisted on buying a round of drinks. They left a few untouched on the bar.

It was now around 7:00 PM and too late to try to get a train to Utica. Bill didn't want to arrive again in the middle of the night. Instead, he took a cab to the Bronx and enjoyed an overnight with the Rowane's. Jack had come home and was back at Rome Air Base, again boarding at Kate's. Tom was at home. Ann and Mr. and Mrs. Rowane greeted Bill warmly. This was the last home he'd visited before going overseas and the first upon arrival back. Being with them felt like his second home.

Bill called the boarding house and talked to Kate, explaining that he would be home late Saturday afternoon.

Early the next morning, Tom went over to Manhattan with Bill to Larry's home. It was a pleasure meeting his family. For an early lunch, his mother had prepared a mini-banquet. Fortunately, there was no anisette in sight, but plenty of homemade wine. They asked Bill to stay overnight for a big welcome home party for Larry. Bill begged off but promised to visit in April.

It was a quick trip to Grand Central Station. The NYCRR train looked fantastic. It was sleek and ready to travel. It was mostly an overcast Saturday afternoon traveling along the Hudson and later into the Mohawk Valley. Bill couldn't help recalling his conversation with Lou Novak back in July of 1943 as they traveled to Camp Upton.

Finally, it was announced, "Station stop, Utica."

Bill's brothers John, Martin and James were waiting on the train platform. Bill O'Connor was with them. They were all wound up. Apparently, they had been doing a little celebrating earlier that afternoon. They thought it a good idea to stop at their favorite bar on the way home but Bill insisted on getting along. They drove along in Bill O'Connor's Chrysler.

It was not necessary to ring the doorbell this time. Kate was watching in the front window. It was simply a great feeling to be home once again and to greet everyone.

Dinner had been prepared. Kate looked a little more tired than Bill remembered. She announced that they were, in effect, late for dinner and to be seated. Jack Rowane, Tim Smiddy, Fred Freeman and the others had a hundred questions. Bill was the last to finish dinner. Roast beef with mashed potatoes, vegetable, homemade biscuits and, of course, Kate had made four or five beautiful apple pies just for the occasion.

The surroundings in the house reminded Bill of the boarding house of yesteryear. There was an air of serenity throughout and it seemed so far removed from recent world events. The people at dinner began talking all at once about events, new cars and the upcoming season of baseball. Kate stepped in and gave orders to finish up since she still had to clean up the room.

She would not let Bill help her in the kitchen after dinner. Instead, she took him to his old bedroom for a surprise homecoming gift. She had purchased a beautiful cherry desk with four drawers on each side.

That evening, Jack Rowane and Bill visited St. John's Church for Confession. Bill sat for awhile in the quietness of the church. It was so peaceful and serene and so unlike the makeshift altars and temporary religious settings he had experienced since 1943. The church had only a few lights on. One of these was a spotlight shining on an enormous cross on the left side wall. Bill had envisioned that cross many times while he was away.

The Stanley Theater had a good movie that night. The place never looked better. The evening wouldn't have been complete without a trip to the diner for hamburgers and coffee. And they never tasted better.

Kate and Bill attended the 7:00 Mass the next morning and then it was home for breakfast. Sunday was spent visiting Catherine and Bill and little Kathleen along with the rest of the family. Everyone looked fine. All of the nieces and nephews were much taller.

The first week home turned out to be most unusual and required a bit of an adjustment. The relaxed schedule was welcomed after a steady diet of formations, schedules, ships and trains. In fact, it seemed to Bill that he should be going somewhere or following an itinerary. But there were no requirements on his time. He began helping Kate at the house and with the shopping. In some ways, it seemed almost like earlier times.

Bill began making plans to find work. He also gave some thought to college. This, however, would require some funding and a move away, which he did not think was currently feasible. He talked to Kate about a full or partial retirement from the work schedule she had maintained for so many years. Being independent all her life, Kate let Bill know in a nice way that she planned to keep going. "I do not want to sit in anyone's corner," she told him.

While in search of work, Bill took advantage of a veteran's benefit. He went to the New York State Unemployment Office and signed for the "52-20" club. As he looked for a job, he would be paid $20.00 per week up to 52 weeks. However, after the third week of signing, Bill felt so embarrassed, he doubled his efforts in searching for a job.

Meantime, Larry Palladino asked Bill down for an

April weekend. This was to be a reunion for all of Larry's family. Bill rode the train for a great time with Larry and his family. He also met a few of the old 458th QMC group.

The following week, Bill purchased a well-used 1933 Ford. It was intended for in-city use only, preferably sticking close to the bus routes. This car burned more oil than gasoline. When a traffic light went from red to green and Bill started up, the smoke screen behind the Ford blocked out all traffic. He quietly sold the car. It was back to riding the bus.

A temporary job came along working in a factory manufacturing bicycle wheels. The job was no challenge but the paycheck was welcomed.

Starting in early May, Kate began to have stomach problems. The doctors concluded it was her appendix. She was scheduled for surgery.

After the operation, Kate seemed to start to bounce back but then complications set in. She was confined to her bed. Again, after consulting with her physician, she was admitted to St. Elizabeth Hospital. It became necessary to perform an operation to relieve a blockage. Following this operation, her surgeon, Dr. Fred Miller, went to the family and was saddened to inform them that Kate was in the advanced stages of cancer. It was going to be a case of keeping her comfortable.

Kate was now unable to speak to her family but would follow each around the hospital room with her eyes. Bill was alone with her on June 11 when she passed away peacefully. A bright light had been extinguished in many people's lives.

Kate had always set the example through her courage in hard times, supporting her ill husband, working against impossible odds to feed and raise her family while helping others who had even less than she. Kate never hesitated to put herself last. Her family always came first.

Although deeply saddened, the family was relieved that Kate was now at rest and no longer in pain.

Bill O'Connor and Catherine helped Bill with the arrangements. The wake was held at home with family, friends and relatives nearby. Bill noticed that there were only a handful of the "Irish Old Timers" in attendance. Following the Funeral Mass at St. John's Church, Kate was laid to rest at Mount Olivet alongside her husband James, daughter Mary and infant son James.

On the afternoon of the visitations, Bill was introduced to a young lady, Cecelia Donovan, who had accompanied her brother James. Bill knew that he would make every effort to try and follow up this initial meeting.

The boarding house arrangement was over. Bill told the boarders they could stay on since he planned to live there for an indefinite period. Meals would be taken elsewhere. A housekeeper would be hired.

And now, the family was down to one. Still saddened by the loss of Kate so soon after arriving back home, Bill nevertheless was glad he chose to leave the Army and get home with her, even for only a few months.

The future beckoned with opportunities for Bill including schooling, a challenging career and hopefully, a family. It was with these goals in mind that he moved forward confidently, as Kate would expect of him.

POSTSCRIPT

The year 2000 and some 100 years following Kate and Jim's marriage and family, they could never have conceived the enormous changes that have taken place. Long gone is their style of living along with the old homesteads on Bleecker Street and Steuben Street.

"Young" Bill, now 75 years of age, lives with his wife, the former Cecelia (Ceil) Donovan, whom he met in 1946. Married in 1948, they are the proud parents of seven children comprising four daughters: Sheila and Sharon (twins), Shawn and Shannon. The boys include William Jr., Timothy and Michael. There are ten grandchildren.

Following Army service, Bill was employed at various area companies while attending Utica College of Syracuse University Evening Division. He joined General Electric Company, working from 1951 to 1985, holding a Human Resource Management position with the Aerospace Electronics Division. Following retirement, he consulted for GE a few years while pursuing his own HR business.

Prior to marriage, Ceil had been a secretary but set this role aside to care for the household with its challenges from grammar school through a BA or BS degree for all the children. Ceil carries a steady schedule of volunteer work at several community organizations including a nursing home and Historic Old St. John's Church. The children maintain their own homes and reside in New York, Virginia and North Carolina.

The members that comprised Kate and Jim's family have all passed away except for Bill and James.

Although it is always more appropriate to look ahead than back, it is difficult at times to appreciate the great number of relatives and friends, both personal and business, that have come and gone. These were an honest, hard-working and patriotic group, supporting community, church and each other.

All of these fine people were privileged to have enjoyed life in surroundings with freedom guaranteed under the Constitution. Some had served in the military to protect these freedoms, taking nothing for granted.

The grandchildren of today, who are the leaders of tomorrow, need to be impressed by parents and teachers alike on the great importance of citizenship responsibilities.

Such action will help the current system to survive and provide continued freedom for the Kate's and Jim's of tomorrow.

RECIPES

A collection of selected recipes is presented from Kate's cookbook.

The recipes are those that were in vogue during the early 1900's. Most ovens were heated by a wood or coal fired source.

Readers will note instructions to "put in oven one hour." No temperature is suggested. Some recipes instruct to place in a "quick oven" or a "moderate oven". Some trial and error may be required. A timetable for baking is shown.

Calories were not a consideration in early century recipes. Key ingredients include butter, lard, whole milk and plenty of eggs.

TIMETABLE FOR BAKING

Loaf Bread	45 to 60 minutes
Rolls and Biscuits	10 to 20 minutes
Gingerbread	30 minutes
Plain Cake	30 to 40 minutes
Fruit Cake	2 to 3 hours
Cookies	10 to 15 minutes

SOUPS

BEAN SOUP

1 cup dried beans, 3 1/2 qts. water.

Soak overnight, then drain off the water. Add 2 qts. fresh water and let beans simmer slowly until very soft. Press through a sieve and if necessary add milk or water to make it the consistency of white sauce. Mix 2 tablespoons butter, 2 of flour, until blended and stir into the soup, cooking and stirring until thick. Remove from fire and add 1 Steero Bouillon Cube dissolved in 1 cup boiling water. Season to taste.

CREAM OF MUSHROOM SOUP

2 tablespoons flour, 2 tablespoons butter, 1 tablespoon beef extract, 1 pint hot water, 1 can mushrooms, 1 qt. cream.

Cook flour and butter until smooth. Add beef extract and hot water. Let it simmer and then add mushrooms, sliced, and liquor from them. Heat the cream in a double boiler, add to the first mixture, season to taste and serve at once. This is sufficient for 12 persons.

OYSTER SOUP

2 qts. oysters, 1 qt. milk, 2 tablespoons butter, 1 cup hot water, seasoning.

Strain all liquor from oysters; add water, and heat. When near boiling, add the seasoning, then the oysters. Cook about 5 minutes or until they ruffle. Stir in the butter, cook 1 minute and pour into the tureen. Stir in the boiling milk and send to table.

NOODLES

Beat 1 egg light, add a pinch of salt and flour enough to make a very stiff dough; roll out very thin, like thin pie crust, dredge with flour to keep from sticking. Let it remain on the bread board to dry for an hour or more; then roll it up into a tight scroll, like a sheet of music. Begin at the end and slice it into slips as thin as straws. After all are cut, mix them lightly together and to prevent them from sticking, keep them floured a little until you are ready to drop them into your soup.

CROUTONS

Cut stale bread in 1/3 inch slices and remove crusts. Spread thinly with butter. Cut slices in 1/3 inch cubes, put in pan and bake until delicately brown, or fry in deep fat.

FISH

OYSTER DRESSING FOR FISH

1 pt. Oysters, 1 cup bread crumbs, seasoned and buttered. Drain and roll each oyster in the crumbs. Fill the fish with the oysters and sprinkle the remainder of the crumbs over the oysters.

CREAMED FISH FLAKES ON TOAST

Melt 2 tablespoonfuls of butter; in it cook 2 tablespoons of flour and 1/4 teaspoonful of pepper; add 1 cupful of milk and stir until boiling. Add a can of fish flakes, cover, and let stand to become very hot. Turn upon slices of toast, softened on the edges in boiling water and buttered; or serve with hot baked potatoes. The beaten yolk of an egg may be added just before pouring over the toast, or the yolk of a "hard-cooked" egg may be sifted over the fish on the toast. For a more substantial dish, set a poached egg above the fish on each slice of toast.

OYSTER COCKTAIL (Individual Recipe)
4 raw oysters, 1/2 tablespoon catsup, 1 teaspoon lemon juice, 1/4 teaspoon Worcestershire, 1 teaspoon chopped celery, Tabasco sauce, salt.

Mix ingredients; chill thoroughly, and serve in cocktail glasses.

SHRIMP WIGGLE
1 can French peas, 1 can shrimps, 1 cup light cream.
Let peas come to a boil in their own liquor. Strain and add to the cream. Break up the shrimps and add to the peas. When shrimps are warmed through, serve on toast or crackers.

CREAMED TUNA FISH
Make cream sauce from 2 rounding tablespoons each butter and flour, 1 3/4 cups milk; season with 1/2 teaspoon pepper to taste and a few grains, if liked, of onion or celery salt. When sauce is well cooked add 1 large can flaked tuna. Stir lightly with fork to keep tuna dainty in appearance and heat slowly until ready to serve. Especially nice served with French fried or baked potatoes. Garnish with finely cut parsley or chopped hard boiled eggs.

DEVILED CRABS
1 cup milk, 2 tablespoons flour, 2 tablespoons butter.

Mash yolks of 2 hard boiled eggs, mix with pint crab meat; season with salt, paprika, and parsley. Stir into the sauce, sprinkle top with egg and bread crumbs.

SALMON LOAF

1 can salmon (shredded), 1 egg, 3/4 cup bread crumbs, 2 teaspoons melted butter, salt and pepper.

Form into a loaf and steam 30 minutes. Serve with sauce made as follows: 1 tablespoon flour, 2 tablespoons melted butter, pinch of salt. Cream together and add enough boiling water to make a sauce of right consistency.

MADRAS BAKED HALIBUT

Season a halibut or any desired white fish with salt, pepper, ginger and curry powder. Place in a baking pan with 1 sliced onion, 2 chopped green peppers and a sprig of parsley. Pour over two tablespoonfuls of melted butter and 1 cupful of hot water. Sprinkle with flour and bake until a delicate brown. Garnish with lemon slices, parsley or mint.

FISH FLAKES A LA MEXICANA

A cup and a half of canned tomatoes, half a green or red pepper (cut in shreds), a slice of onion and 1/4 teaspoonful of salt; simmer 15 minutes; press through a sieve, add a tablespoonful of butter and a can of fish flakes. Let stand over the fire to become very hot. Serve with boiled rice.

MEATS

IRISH STEW

1/2 lb. veal, 1/2 lb. beef, 1/2 lb. lamb, 1/4 lb. salt pork.

Put over the fire 2 hours before dinner. At the end of 1 hour add 2 carrots, 1/2 cup chopped celery, 4 onions, and parsley, thyme, summer savory, bay leaves, at discretion. 30 minutes before serving, add some thinly cut potatoes, seasoned to taste and thicken slightly.

VEAL LOAF

3 lbs. raw veal, 1/2 lb. raw ham or pork, 6 crackers (rolled), 4 teaspoons cream, 2 tablespoons lemon juice, 1 tablespoon salt, 1/2 tablespoon pepper.

Chop meats, mix together and add crackers and other ingredients, and also a little onion juice. Pack in a small bread-pan and brush over with 1/2 cup boiling water in which has been melted 2 tablespoons butter. Cool and cut in thin slices for serving.

SUPPER-DISH

1 cup cold boiled rice, 1 cup chopped beef, 1 can tomatoes, 1 small onion, chopped.

Mix all together, season with butter, pepper and salt. Put bread or cracker crumbs and bits of butter over the top and bake in a brisk oven from 1/2 to 3/4 hour.

ITALIAN STEW

2 lbs. beef (stewing piece), 1/2 can tomatoes, 3 green or red peppers, seasoning.

Cover the beef with water and cook 1 hour. Then add tomatoes and cook until tender. Then add the peppers sliced, cook and season to taste.

MEAT OMELET

Mix any pieces of cold meat, add a few bread crumbs or cracker crumbs and enough beaten egg to bind them together. Season well and pour into a well-buttered frying pan.

HUNGARIAN GOULASH

2 lbs. round steak, 2 large onions, 1/4 head cabbage, 2 carrots, 1 small turnip, 6 medium sized potatoes, 1 can tomatoes, 1/2 cup pearl tapioca.

Cut steak into pieces 2 in. square and put into a roasting pan; cut carrots into cubes; slice onions and cut turnips into cubes; add to the meat in layers after sprinkling the meat with salt and pepper. Slice cabbage fine; add to other vegetables. Soak tapioca in cold water for 5 minutes and then spread over all with a tablespoon. Add potatoes pared and cut the size of an English walnut. Cover with tomatoes. Add a few dashes of Worcestershire sauce, butter, pepper and salt. Put cover on and cook in moderate oven from 1 to 2 hours. This is sufficient for 6 people.

SPANISH RICE

1 1/2 pounds of ground beefsteak, cup of cooked rice, 1 onion fried. Then add to steak and rice 1 can of tomatoes, a little salt and chili powder. Sprinkle cracker crumbs on top and dot with butter. Bake an hour.

MEAT AND FISH SAUCES

CREAM HORSERADISH SAUCE FOR COLD HAM

1/2 cup sour cream (beaten), 1/2 teaspoon salt, 1 teaspoon sugar, 1/2 cup grated horseradish.

Add salt and sugar to the beaten cream and then beat in horseradish.

HOLLANDAISE SAUCE

1/2 cup butter, 3 egg yolks, 1/2 lemon (juice), 1/2 teaspoon salt, cayenne pepper.

Rub butter to a cream and beat eggs and butter well. Add slowly 1 cup hot water, mix well and set it into a saucepan of hot water. Stir constantly until it becomes thick like cream. Do not let it boil.

COCKTAIL SAUCE FOR OYSTERS AND CLAMS
1 can tomatoes, 1 teaspoon pepper, 1 teaspoon mustard, 1/2 cup vinegar, 1/4 teaspoon allspice, 1/4 teaspoon cinnamon, 1/2 tablespoon salt.

Cook slowly for 2 hours; then rub through a sieve. When serving add a little chopped celery or grated horseradish.

APPLE SAUCE
2 qts. apples, 1 1/2 cups sugar.

Pare and quarter the apples; add sugar and enough water to cover and cook slowly in a double boiler. Add vanilla and a little nutmeg.

MINT SAUCE
1/4 cup finely chopped mint leaves, 1/2 teaspoon salt, 1 tablespoon powdered sugar, 1/2 cup mild vinegar.

SAUCE TARTARE
1 cup mayonnaise dressing, 1 tablespoon chopped pickled cucumbers, tablespoon chopped olives, 1 tablespoon chopped capers. Mix well.

BREADS

CORN BREAD
3 tablespoons shortening, 1 egg, 1 cup sweet milk, 1 cup flour, 1 cup corn meal, 3 teaspoons baking powder, 1 tablespoon sugar, 1 pinch of salt.

Beat well and bake in quick oven.

OATMEAL BREAD
4 cups oatmeal, 8 cups boiling water, 1 cup molasses, 1 tablespoon salt, 1 yeast cake, flour.

Pour boiling water over oatmeal and let stand until cool; add yeast cake dissolved in warm water, molasses, salt and enough flour to make a stiff batter; knead it with a little flour; allow it to rise. Mold into loaves; allow to rise again and bake 1 hour.

NUT BREAD
4 cups sifted flour, 4 teaspoons baking powder, 1 teaspoon salt.

Sift together, then add 2 cups milk, 1 egg, 1 cup brown sugar, 1 cup chopped nut meats. Bake half hour.

SCONES
1 qt. flour, 1/2 lb. butter, 2 eggs, 3 teaspoons baking powder. Rub butter into flour with baking powder, a little salt and sugar. Put eggs into mixture without beating. Mix stiff enough to roll, cut, add a little milk if needed, roll 1/2 inch thick and cut in triangles. Sprinkle with sugar and bake 20 minutes.

BAKING POWDER BISCUITS
1 3/4 cups flour, 1 1/2 heaping teaspoons baking powder, 1/2 teaspoon salt, 1 teaspoon sugar, 2 tablespoons shortening, 1 cup milk.

Sift all dry ingredients together; then rub in shortening. Add milk. Roll out using as little flour as possible and handling the dough no more than is absolutely necessary. Cut and bake from 20 to 30 minutes in a hot oven.

PIES

1-2-3 PIE CRUST
1 cup flour, 2 tablespoons lard, 3 tablespoons water, 1 pinch salt.

OLD-FASHIONED APPLE PIE

Peel and core moderately tart and ripe apples; Baldwin, Russets and Greenings are excellent. Cut them into thin slices, fill under crust; then sprinkle over them brown sugar or pour over them molasses to sweeten sufficiently. Lay over the upper crust and bake in a moderate oven about 40 minutes.

CUSTARD PIE

3 eggs, 1 pint milk, 4 heaping tablespoons sugar; nutmeg; salt, 1/2 teaspoon flour.

Bake until free from knife.

COCONUT PIE

Same as custard pie; add 1/2 fresh coconut, grated.

CHERRY PIE

Line your pie-plate with good crust; fill half full with ripe cherries; sprinkle over them a cupful of sugar, a teaspoon of sifted flour, dot a few bits of butter over that. Now fill the crust full to the top. Cover with the upper crust and bake.

PUMPKIN PIE

1 cup pumpkin, 1/2 cup sugar, 2 cups milk, 1/2 teaspoon ginger, 1/2 teaspoon cinnamon, 2 eggs.

Beat the eggs and add to them sugar, pumpkin and spices. Beat thoroughly and then add the milk. Mix thoroughly and bake in raw crust.

DESSERTS

JELL-O WITH FRUIT

Dissolve 1 package of Jell-O, any flavor, in a pint of boiling water. Pour into a bowl or mold. Just as Jell-O is beginning to set, arrange in it, with the aid of a fork, sliced oranges and bananas or peaches and strawberries or cherries and currants or any other fruit that may be preferred for the purpose.

HOT WATER GINGERBREAD
1 cup molasses, 1/4 cup boiling water, 2 cups flour, 1 teaspoon soda, 1 1/2 teaspoons ginger, 1/2 teaspoon salt, 4 tablespoons melted butter.

Add water to molasses. Mix and sift dry ingredients, combine mixtures, add butter, and beat vigorously. Pour into a buttered shallow pan, and bake 25 minutes in a moderate oven.

FRIED CAKES
1 cup sugar, butter size of a walnut, 2 eggs, 1 cup milk, 3 teaspoons baking powder, flour.

Cream sugar and butter; add eggs and beat all thoroughly. Then add milk and flour and baking powder. Make the dough no stiffer than is necessary to roll. Roll, cut and fry in deep grease.

MOLASSES COOKIES
2 cups molasses, 1 cup sugar, 1 cup lard, 1 cup hot water, 7 1/2 cups flour, 4 teaspoons baking powder, 1 teaspoon salt, 1 teaspoon ginger.

Mix well and let stand over night. In the morning, roll and cut and bake in quick oven.

SOFT SUGAR COOKIES
1 cup butter, 2 cups sugar, 2 eggs, 1/2 teaspoon salt, 1 cup milk, 4 cups flour, 3 teaspoons baking powder, 1 teaspoon lemon or vanilla extract.

Cream butter, add sugar. When creamy add other ingredients. Chill. Roll, cut in rounds and bake in a quick oven.

CAKES

SOUR CREAM CAKE
1 cup sour cream, 1 cup sugar, 1 egg, a little nutmeg, 1 teaspoon soda (scant), 2 small cups flour.

Bake rather slowly.

SPICE CAKE
3 eggs, 1 cup butter or half butter and lard, 2 cups sugar, 1 cup sour milk, 1 cup raisins, 1 teaspoon cinnamon, 1 teaspoon cloves, 1/2 teaspoon grated nutmeg, 1 teaspoon soda dissolved in a little hot water, 3 cups flour.

APPLESAUCE CAKE
1 cup sugar, 1/2 cup butter, 1 1/2 cups apple sauce, 1 teaspoon soda dissolved in a little hot water, 1/2 teaspoon cloves, 1/2 teaspoon cinnamon, 1 cup chopped raisins, 2 cups flour; salt, vanilla.

Bake slowly in moderate oven.

COCOA CAKE
1 cup sugar, 2 egg yolks, 2 level tablespoons butter, 1 cup sour milk, 1/2 cup dry cocoa, 1 level teaspoon soda, 1 1/2 cups flour, 1 teaspoon vanilla.

Bake in a moderate oven.

FRUIT CAKE
5 eggs well beaten, 1/2 lb. butter, 1 cup milk, 1 cup molasses, 2 cups brown sugar, 1 wineglass brandy, 1/2 teaspoon salt, 1 teaspoon saleratus, 1 teaspoon each of cloves, cinnamon, allspice, nutmeg, mace, 1 sifter flour, raisins, currants, citron.

Bake in a moderate oven 2 1/2 hours.

CHEAP FRUIT CAKE

2 eggs, 3/4 cup sugar, 1/2 cup molasses, 3/4 cup sour milk, 1 teaspoon baking soda (scant), 2 cups flour into which stir 1 teaspoon cinnamon, 1/2 teaspoon allspice, 1/4 teaspoon cloves and a little grated nutmeg, 2 cups seeded raisins, 1 cup chopped walnuts, a little citron.

Bake in fairly hot oven for 3/4 hour. Makes two loaves.

BOILED FROSTING

1 cup granulated sugar, 1/2 cup boiling water poured over it.

Cook until it threads. Stir slowly into the beaten white of 1 egg. Flavor and beat well.

FUDGE

BROWN SUGAR FUDGE

1 lb. brown sugar, 1/4 cup milk, 1/4 cup maple syrup, 1 tablespoon butter.

Boil until it forms a soft ball in water. Stir and when it begins to grain, add nuts, pour into buttered tins and mark into squares.

CHOCOLATE FUDGE

2 cups granulated sugar, 9 teaspoons cocoa, 1 teaspoon butter, 3/4 cup milk.

Boil until it forms a soft ball in cold water. Then add vanilla and nuts and stir until it begins to thicken. Pour on a buttered platter to cool.

WELLESLEY FUDGE

1 cup sugar, 1 cup milk, butter size of an egg, 4 heaping

teaspoons cocoa, 1 teaspoon vanilla.

Boil about 20 minutes or until a little dropped in cold water will form a soft ball. Spread on buttered tins or plate and mark off into squares.

PEANUT BRITTLE
Put 2 cupfuls of granulated sugar in a frying pan over a hot fire and stir constantly until quite brown. Add 1 cup- ful of chopped peanuts, stir in through the sugar and turn into a buttered pan.